CIHM
Microfiche
Series
(Monographs)

ICMH
Collection de
microfiches
(monographies)

Canadian Institute for Historical Microreproductions / Institut canadien de microreproductions historiques

Technical and Bibliographic Notes / Notes techniques et bibliographiques

The Institute has attempted to obtain the best original copy available for filming. Features of this copy which may be bibliographically unique, which may alter any of the images in the reproduction, or which may significantly change the usual method of filming, are checked below.

L'Institut a microfilmé le meilleur exemplaire qu'il lui a été possible de se procurer. Les détails de cet exemplaire qui sont peut-être uniques du point de vue bibliographique, qui peuvent modifier une image reproduite, ou qui peuvent exiger une modification dans la méthode normale de filmage sont indiqués ci-dessous.

- [ ] Coloured covers/
  Couverture de couleur

- [ ] Covers damaged/
  Couverture endommagée

- [ ] Covers restored and/or laminated/
  Couverture restaurée et/ou pelliculée

- [ ] Cover title missing/
  Le titre de couverture manque

- [ ] Coloured maps/
  Cartes géographiques en couleur

- [ ] Coloured ink (i.e. other than blue or black)/
  Encre de couleur (i.e. autre que bleue ou noire)

- [ ] Coloured plates and/or illustrations/
  Planches et/ou illustrations en couleur

- [ ] Bound with other material/
  Relié avec d'autres documents

- [x] Tight binding may cause shadows or distortion along interior margin/
  La reliure serrée peut causer de l'ombre ou de la distorsion le long de la marge intérieure

- [ ] Blank leaves added during restoration may appear within the text. Whenever possible, these have been omitted from filming/
  Il se peut que certaines pages blanches ajoutées lors d'une restauration apparaissent dans le texte, mais, lorsque cela était possible, ces pages n'ont pas été filmées.

- [ ] Additional comments:/
  Commentaires supplémentaires:

- [ ] Coloured pages/
  Pages de couleur

- [ ] Pages damaged/
  Pages endommagées

- [ ] Pages restored and/or laminated/
  Pages restaurées et/ou pelliculées

- [x] Pages discoloured, stained or foxed/
  Pages décolorées, tachetées ou piquées

- [ ] Pages detached/
  Pages détachées

- [x] Showthrough/
  Transparence

- [ ] Quality of print varies/
  Qualité inégale de l'impression

- [ ] Continuous pagination/
  Pagination continue

- [x] Includes index(es)/
  Comprend un (des) index

  Title on header taken from:/
  Le titre de l'en-tête provient:

- [ ] Title page of issue/
  Page de titre de la livraison

- [ ] Caption of issue/
  Titre de départ de la livraison

- [ ] Masthead/
  Générique (périodiques) de la livraison

This item is filmed at the reduction ratio checked below/
Ce document est filmé au taux de réduction indiqué ci-dessous.

10X	14X	18X	22X	26X	30X
12X	16X	20X	24X	28X	32X

The copy filmed here has been reproduced thanks to the generosity of:

University of Alberta
Edmonton

The images appearing here are the best quality possible considering the condition and legibility of the original copy and in keeping with the filming contract specifications.

Original copies in printed paper covers are filmed beginning with the front cover and ending on the last page with a printed or illustrated impression, or the back cover when appropriate. All other original copies are filmed beginning on the first page with a printed or illustrated impression, and ending on the last page with a printed or illustrated impression.

The last recorded frame on each microfiche shall contain the symbol → (meaning "CONTINUED"), or the symbol ▽ (meaning "END"), whichever applies.

Maps, plates, charts, etc., may be filmed at different reduction ratios. Those too large to be entirely included in one exposure are filmed beginning in the upper left hand corner, left to right and top to bottom, as many frames as required. The following diagrams illustrate the method:

L'exemplaire filmé fut reproduit grâce à la générosité de:

University of Alberta
Edmonton

Les images suivantes ont été reproduites avec le plus grand soin, compte tenu de la condition et de la netteté de l'exemplaire filmé, et en conformité avec les conditions du contrat de filmage.

Les exemplaires originaux dont la couverture en papier est imprimée sont filmés en commençant par le premier plat et en terminant soit par la dernière page qui comporte une empreinte d'impression ou d'illustration, soit par le second plat, selon le cas. Tous les autres exemplaires originaux sont filmés en commençant par la première page qui comporte une empreinte d'impression ou d'illustration et en terminant par la dernière page qui comporte une telle empreinte.

Un des symboles suivants apparaîtra sur la dernière image de chaque microfiche, selon le cas: le symbole → signifie "A SUIVRE", le symbole ▽ signifie "FIN".

Les cartes, planches, tableaux, etc., peuvent être filmés à des taux de réduction différents. Lorsque le document est trop grand pour être reproduit en un seul cliché, il est filmé à partir de l'angle supérieur gauche, de gauche à droite, et de haut en bas, en prenant le nombre d'images nécessaire. Les diagrammes suivants illustrent la méthode.

1	2	3

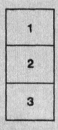

1	2	3
4	5	6

MICROCOPY RESOLUTION TEST CHART

(ANSI and ISO TEST CHART No. 2)

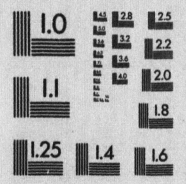

 APPLIED IMAGE Inc

1653 East Main Street
Rochester, New York   14609   USA
(716) 482 - 0300 - Phone
(716) 288 - 5989 - Fax

A STUDY OF THE THLINGETS
OF ALASKA

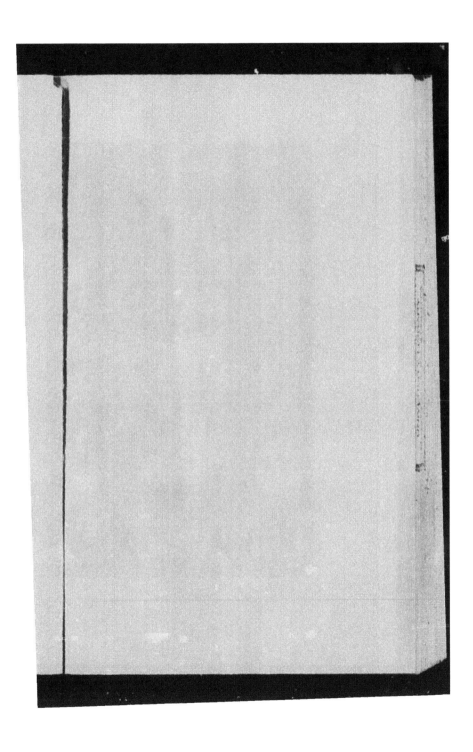

" LOVERS' WALK "

A Study of the Thlingets of Alaska

By

LIVINGSTON F. JONES

NEW YORK   CHICAGO   TORONTO
Fleming H. Revell Company
LONDON   AND   EDINBURGH

New York: 158 Fifth Avenue
Chicago: 125 N. Wabash Ave.
Toronto: 25 Richmond St., W.
London: 21 Paternoster Square
Edinburgh: 100 Princes Street

PREFACE

MANY books have been written on Alaska. In nearly all of them something has been said about the natives, or aborigines, of the country. In some they are merely alluded to, while in others they are treated more or less comprehensively. While some are reliable so far as they go, others abound with errors and contain statements about the natives which are not true. The same may be said about many articles that have appeared in various periodicals.

It is evident to those who are intimately acquainted with the natives, that some writers have come to their work with little or no preparation. In truth, several of the books extant on Alaska, as well as scores of articles which have appeared in periodicals, have been written by tourists who had but limited opportunities of studying the natives and their customs.

Some of the books, and not a few of the articles, were written on " hurry-up " orders, and by persons who had merely glanced at the country from the deck of a passing steamer. Hearsay and idle rumour furnished much of their contents. Some of them contain fake stories. Had their authors been more intent on publishing facts than on breaking into print such stories would never have been set up in cold type. A novelist may have some license in printing fiction, but he who purports to be telling the truth should know whereof he speaks.

While there are several reliable works on Alaska in which much may be found concerning the lives of the aborigines, yet even more of interest has been left unsaid. For this reason the author feels his effort justified in order to give fuller and more accurate information to the public concerning these interesting people.

Again, while this work treats almost exclusively of the Thlingets of Alaska, yet what is said of them largely applies to the other classes.

The information imparted to the public in the following pages has been gleaned by the writer almost entirely from the natives themselves, either through their lips or by his own personal observation. Having lived and laboured among them for more than twenty years, he has had exceptional opportunities of studying their customs and characteristics. He has read the books and articles appearing in periodicals relating to the natives. (Few exist that he has not read.) These were consulted not so much for information—he preferred to get that at first hand—as to see what others had to say about the Alaskan and wherein they confirmed his own findings or differed with him.

It has proved to the author a most fascinating study, and while necessarily there has been some drudgery connected with the preparation of the work, on the whole it has been one of extreme pleasure. It is now offered to the public in the full consciousness that long and painstaking care has been given to its preparation, and if while not free from imperfections such errors are not there through slight.

L. F. J.

JUNEAU, ALASKA.

I. INT

I
C
ip
m
K
qu

II. ABO

Na
ful
Th
Tw
Su
in

III. ORI

Dif
can
Pro
Fav
of
men
Test
—J
tom
and

IV. THE

No v
Gene
Word

CONTENTS

I. INTRODUCTORY 17

Important Factors in the Lives of a People — The
Country — Name — Area — Physical Features — Archipelago — Channels — Mountains — Distance — Climate — Mistaken Ideas — Climate Diversified —
Kuro-Siwo Current — Vegetation — Resources — Requirements to Obtain Them — Industries.

II. ABORIGINES OF ALASKA 23

Native Population — Four Grand Divisions — Fanci-
ful Divisions — Different Types of Language — The
Thlingets — Their Villages — Their Tribes — The
Two Great Totemic Divisions (Crow and Eagle) —
Sub-division into Clans and Families — Difference
in Dialect and Disposition.

III. ORIGIN OF THE ALASKANS 27

Different Theories Concerning Origin — The Mexican Theory — The North American Indian Theory —
Prof. Wm. H. Dall's Position — Arguments in
Favour of the Mongolian Theory — The Consensus
of Opinion — The Author's Position — His Arguments in Support of the Mongolian Theory — The
Testimony of Early Russians — Of Various Writers
— J. W. Arctander's Position — Similarity of Customs and Personal Resemblance Between Alaskans
and Islanders — The Author's Deduction.

V. THE THLINGET LANGUAGE 35

No Written Language — Handed down Orally from
Generation to Generation — Many Words Obsolete —
Word-building — Corruptions — Borrowed Words —

Chinook — Proper Names — Fathers Changing Name
on Birth of First Child — Names Belonging to Certain Tribes — Extent of the Thlinget Vocabulary —
Abstract and Concrete Terms — Peculiarities of the
Language — Deficiency of the Language Illustrated —
Peculiarity of the Language When Spoken — Grammatical Construction — Verbs — Gender — Structure
of Sentences — Observation of the Author as to the
Desirability of English over Thlinget.

V. THE FAMILY 44

Relation of Husband and Wife — Of Children to
Parents — Treatment of Nephews and Nieces by
Uncles and Aunts — The Fondness of Parents for
Children — Illegitimate — Childbirth — Treatment
of Babes — Weaning Children — Parental Indulgence
of Children — Polyandry — Domestic Life — Cooking — Rovings — Dogs — Washing and Sewing —
Gossiping — Quarrels — Status of Wife — No Servants — Exceptions to Poor Housekeepers — Drawbacks to be Remembered.

VI. THE COMMUNITY 53

Communities Independent — The Only Bond — Where
Built — Advantages — Construction — Status of Na-
tive — Early Building — Handicaps Years Ago — Ad-
vantages and Improvements Now — Summer Camps
— The Composition of Each Community — Public
Utilities — Sanitary Conditions — The More Pro-
gressive Natives — Social Life — Strata of Thlinget
Society — Caste — The Chief — Change Communities
Are Constantly Undergoing — Mixture of Whites
and Natives.

VII. PERSONAL APPEARANCE, DRESS AND
ORNAMENTATION 64

Personal Appearance — Dress — Public Appearance
— Dress in Earlier Times — Female Headgear —
Finery for Fourth of July — Good Taste Acquired —
Ornamentation — Jewellery — The Labret — By
Whom Worn — Tattooing — Face Painting — Dress
Ornamentation — Personal Carriage — Facial Looks
— Standard of Beauty — Affiliation with Whites.

VIII. INDUSTRIES 72

Thlingets Self-supporting — Limited Industries —
Main Industry, Fishing — Process of Catching Fish
— Work in Canneries — Employment in Mines —
Hunting and Trapping — Packing Supplies — Carv-
ing in Wood and Metals — The Trades — Industries
for Women — Chilkat Blankets — Canoe-building —
War-canoes — Canoe-racing — Commercial Activi-
ties — Capitalists — The Hydaburg Enterprise —
Drawbacks to Commercial Life.

IX. BASKETRY 85

Female Industry — Time and Labour Required to
Prepare the Materials — Trade and Prices — Quality
of Weaving — Lieut. G. T. Emmons on Basketry —
Names of Baskets According to Design, Weave,
Materials Used and Shape — Weights and Measures
— Sizes of Baskets — Names According to What
They Are Used For — Baskets for Cooking —
Mother-of-Baskets — Colourings — Care Needed in
Splitting Fibres — Tools Used — Position of Basket-
weavers — Weaving — Vending Baskets.

X. TRAITS 92

Independence — Vanity — Sensitiveness — Things Regarded as Shameful and Disgraceful — Revengeful
— Jealousy — Crafty — Politic — Not Avaricious —
Spendthrifts — Fickle — Unreliable — Undemonstrative — Fortitude — Affection for Kindred — Hospitality — Sociability — Fond of Amusements — Observant — Fluency of Speech — Gratitude.

XI. FOOD 103

Liberal Endowment of Food — Fish, the Principal
Food — Varieties — Salmon — Halibut — Herring —
Fish for Oils — Oolikan — Herring Spawn — Salmon
Roe — Delicacies — ʹ ɑd Animals — Fowl — Shell-
fish — Berries — Vegetables — Seaweed — White
Man's Food.

XII. EXTINCT CUSTOMS 112

Customs Divided into Three Classes — First, Obsolete Customs — War — Motives for War — Warriors — Methods of Warfare — Prisoners of War — War with Aleuts, Sticks and Russians — The Famous Chief, Katlian — The Wrangell and Sitka Massacres — Attacks on Russians Justified — Jealous Feuds — Implements of War — Slavery — Extent of Slavery — Treatment of Slaves — Manumission of Slaves — Cremation — Belief Concerning the Burning of the Dead — Polygamy — The Toughening Process — Infanticide — Tattooing — Gambling — Gambling Pegs and Method of Playing — The Game Called Nagon — Other Games.

XIII. WANING CUSTOMS 125

Waning Customs — Witchcraft — Marriage — Methods — The Dowry — Barriers to Marriage — Marrying Blood Relations — Marrying out of Respect to the Wishes of the Dying — Levirate Marriages — Child Marriages — Love-matches — Rules Pertaining to Marriage — Trial Before Marriage — Miscegenation — Seizure of Property Custom — The Custom of Confining Girls When Approaching Womanhood.

XIV. PRESENT-DAY CUSTOMS 135

The Native Feast — Events Calling for Feasts — Obligations Discharged at Feasts — Guests — Commemorative Feasts — Other Feasts — The Potlatch — Motive for Giving Potlatch — Amount Given Away — Dancing in Connection with Feasts — The Attendance — Ceremony on Arrival of Guests — Paraphernalia Used — Period of Time Covered — Rules Governing Potlatches — Dancing — Nature of the Dance — Different Dances — Position and Motions of Dancers — Time, How Kept — Performance Highly Spectacular — The Big Dance at Angoon — The Absurd Custom of Brothers and Sisters Not Speaking to Each Other — The Domination of Custom.

XV. THE DISPOSITION OF THE DEAD . 147

Death Sets in Motion Many Customs — What Fol-
lows the Death of a Chief — Lying in State — The
Widow's Position — Other Mourners — Gathering
Things for the Feast for the Dead — Service of the
Missionary — Burial of Things with the Dead — The
Feast for the Dead — Dressing the Dying for Burial
— Remuneration of Those Who Assist in Any Way —
Grave Fences and Tombstones — Disposition of the
Bodies of Those Lower than Chiefs — In the Days
of Cremation — Thlingets' Fondness for Feasting for
the Dead — Commemorative Feasts — Peculiar Cus-
toms Connected with Burial — Embalming — Burial
Now the Universal Custom — Signs of Mourning.

XVI. SHAMANISM AND SUPERSTITIONS . 154

Witches — The Ikt — The Office of Shaman — Para-
phernalia of Shaman — Propitiation of Evil Spirits
— Compensation of Shaman — The Witch — Treat-
ment of the Witch — Native Terror of Witches —
What the Accusation of Being a Witch Means —
Cases of Witchcraft That Have Come to the Author's
Notice — Witch-medicine — The Superstitious Re-
gard for the Ikt — The Ikt's Burial Place — His
Body Embalmed — Taboos in Connection with the
Ikt — Regarded as a Prophet — Performance of the
Ikt — Other Superstitions — Belief in the Existence
of Evil Spirits — Evil Omens — Taboos — Charms —
Love-potions — Belief in Animals Understanding
Human Speech — Superstition in Regard to Drown-
ing — As to What a Wife Should Do While Hus-
band Is Hunting — In Connection with Births —
Dreams — Supernatural Properties of Medicine —
Superstitions Practised When Fishing.

XVII. TOTEMISM 168

The Subject — Misrepresentations — Totem Poles
Not Idols — Crest — Ko-te-s — Totemic Divisions
— Totemism the Foundation of Entire Social Structure — Origin of Totemism — Marriage and Totemism — Rank and Totemism — Other Things That

Totemism Governs — Totemism Recorded History,
Genealogy, Legend, Memoriam, Commemoration and
Art — Classes of Totem Poles — Totem Pole Work-
manship — Making of Totem Poles a Waning Art
— House Totems or Crests — Clan Emblems — Kok-
won-ton Tribe — The Adoption of Crests.

XVIII. LEGENDS 181

Myths and Legends — Legendary Lore Handed
down Orally — When and by Whom Handed Down
— Purposes of Telling Legends — Legend of Sculpin
— Of the Crow and the Deer — Yalkth, the Creator
— Legend of the Origin of the Mosquito — Of the
Whale Tribe — Of the Beaver Crest — Of the Wolf
Crest — Of the Earthquake — Of the Crow Making
Man — Of the Origin of the Topknot of the Bluejay
— Myth Builders Primitive Philosophers — The
Legend of a Flood — Legends Recounting Thrilling
Events — Attack of the Devilfish — The Totem in
Pioneer Square, Seattle — Legends on House Totems
— Legends Embodied in Songs — Concerning Mt.
Edgecumbe — Concerning Lake Near Kluckwan —
Concerning Madam Skoog-wa.

XIX. NATIVE JURISPRUDENCE . . .193

No Government — No Trials, Courts, Jails, etc.—
Offences Redressed by Tribe — Life for Life — Caste
Determines What Life — Accidental Killing Must
be Atoned for as Well as Intentional Killing —
Instances Cited — Ludicrous Cases — Instances Cited
Where Caste Governs Damages — A Father's Lia-
bility to His Own Child — One Saved from Death
Becomes Slave of His Rescuer — All Loans Bring
100 Per Cent Interest — Motive for Giving — Instances Cited — Exorbitant Charges for Services
About the Dead — Old Grievances Often Revived —
Instances Cited — Chief Has Ruling Voice Concerning Settlements — Thlingets Have Laws and Enforce Them — They Sometimes Ge' Double Punishment.

XX. MUSIC AND AMUSEMENTS . . . 203

Love of Music and Amusements — Singing — Band
Music — Congregational Singing — Native Songs —
Songs Used at Feasts and Potlatches — When Com-
posed — Songs of Recent Composition — The Chant
— Amusements — Games and Athletic Sports —
Socials — The Game of "Ha-goo" — Children Fond
of Toys — Games of Contest — Jokes and Witticisms
— Appreciation of Humour — Amusing Incidents
— The Phonograph at Funeral — Stopping Funeral
Procession for Hearse — Incidents at Weddings —
In Church — How the First Steamboat Was Re-
garded — Their Great Astonishment over the First
Negro Seen — Over Men with Wooden Leg, Wig,
False Teeth, etc.

XXI. MORALITY 212

Different Standards of Morality — That of the Na-
tive and of the White Man Compared — Matters of
Shame and Disgrace with the Thlingets — Un-
just Charges — Difference in Marriage Ceremony —
Care of Daughters — Drunkenness — Soldiers and
Native Debauchery — Rum, the Arch-Evil — Theft
— Murder — Suicide — Abortion — Prostitution —
Truthfulness — Honour — Profanity — Vice — Good
Characters.

XXII. DISEASES 221

Diseases of Recent Introduction — Consumption —
Dr. Paul C. Hutton's Report — Smallpox — Venereal
Diseases — Syphilis — Measles and Whooping-cough
— Original Diseases of Thlingets — Osseous Tuber-
culosis — Ophthalmia — Pott's Disease — Insanity
and Idiocy — Sanitation — Sewerage — Teachers and
Sanitation — Medicines and Remedies — Bleeding
— Treatment of Ulcers and Sores — Use of Natu-
ral Mineral Springs — Steam Bathing — Fasting —
"Rubbers" — Nursing the Sick — The Crying Need
of the Natives — The Climate on Health — Freaks
— Blindness — The Better Class Who Know how to
Care for Themselves.

14 CONTENTS

XXIII. RELIGION 231

The Religious Factor — Not Demonologists — Strictly Speaking, Not Spiritualists — Belief in Spirits — This the Foundation of Shamanism — Ghosts — Not Animal Worshippers — Not Nature Worshippers — Immortality — Transmigration of Soul — Future Place of Soul — Tradition About One Soul Returning — Propitiation of Evil Powers — Originally No Term for God — Their Cosmology — Work of the Russian Church — Protestant Missions — Testimonies to the Work of the Church — Conclusion.

XXIV. EDUCATION 245

The Initial Move in the Education of the Native — The First School Established at Wrangell, 1877 — Schools in Connection with Missions — First Interest Shown by the U. S. Government in the Education of the Natives — Censurable Neglect — A Decade of Feeble Effort — Schools in Various Villages — The Leading Industrial Training School at Sitka Under the Auspices of the Presbyterian Church — Ex-Governor A. P. Swineford's Testimony — The New Up-to-date Mission Plant — The Government's Neglect — Its Effort to Graft Indian Training on to the Ordinary Day School — The Futility of It — Native Aptitude for Trades — Progress They Have Made Despite the Deficient System — Need Opportunities — Reason for Educating Them Here — Their Knowledge of English — What Will Be True of Them a Generation Hence.

INDEX 255

ILLUSTRATIONS

"Lovers' Walk" . . . . *Frontispiece*

OPPOSITE PAGE

Pearl Harbour, Alaska 18

Chilkat and Vicinity 24

Children—"Posing" 44

Auk Village 50

Treadwell Gold Mine 72

Baskets 82

Natives Vending Curios 88

Chilkat Potlatch Dancing 138

Totem Pole 156

Chilkat Blanket and Woman 168

Numerous Curios 178

House Totems and Interesting Objects . . 188

Juneau, Alaska 194

Juneau Native Band 200

A Trout Stream 236

Map of Alaska 254

T

ac
vi
ty
di
the

Ita
re
for

inc
sa
to
re

it
tha
ar
na
"
of
the
the

I

INTRODUCTORY

THE geography, clim and resources of a country are important factors in the lives of its people, as their customs and characteristics are largely determined by their environment. The native of Mexico is a different type of man from the native of C nada; and the difference is largely due to the differences between their respective countries.

This is true even with people of the same race. Italy, with its salubrious climate and agrarian resources, produces a different type from that found in cold and rugged Norway.

In a treatise setting forth the traits, customs, industries and institutions of a people it is necessary, to the better understanding of these things, to first describe their country, its climate and resources. Hence this introductory chapter.

The word " Alaska " has been so often defined it would seem every one must know by this time that it means " Big Country." The term, we are told, is an abbreviation or corruption of the native word Al-ak-sak or Al-ay-ek-sa, meaning " Great Country." * The word Al-ak-shak is not of Thlinget origin, but evidently originated with the Eskimos. It is strikingly appropriate, for the land may well be called " great."

* " Alaska," Sheldon Jackson, page 14.

To say that Alaska has an area of over 617,703 square miles gives but a faint impression of its immensity. It is better understood by comparison. Its area is about equal to the United States east of the Mississippi River.

The coast line of Alaska is even more remarkable than the area. In extent, and probably in its physical features, it surpasses that of any other country on the globe. The physical features of the coast have marked influence on the lives of the Thlingets, making them expert seamen and fishermen.

The part of Alaska occupied by these people is a vast archipelago, containing more than a thousand islands, varying in size from an acre to thousands of square miles.

More villages of the Thlingets are seen on islands than on the mainland. Cozy harbours with fine beaches are chosen for town-sites. As the native is a seafaring man he wants his home at the water's edge. His canoe is always at his door ready for use at a moment's notice.

The islands are mostly mountainous with bold and rocky shores. Pretty beaches are found here and there, but they are not numerous. All of the straits and most of the bays of the archipelago feel the influence of the ocean currents and storms. Some of them are very rough at times and exceedingly dangerous to navigate, yet the natives rove over them at will in their frail canoes. They often go to sea way out of sight of land without compass or chart, yet they find their way back.

A mountain chain fringes the main shore, containing numerous mountains of no mean proportions. Many of them tower thousands of feet into the air and are eternally crowned with snow. Sev-

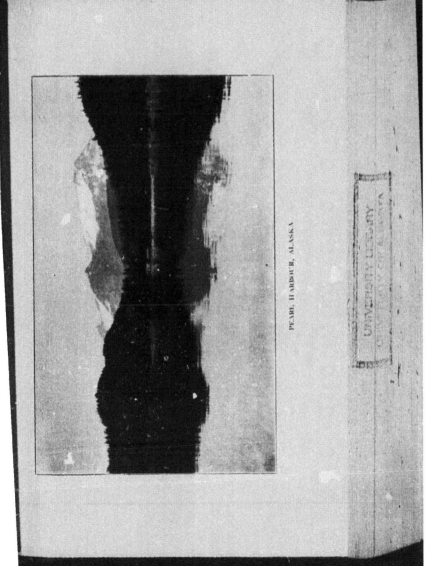

PEARL HARBER, ALASKA

era
ina
Th
tre
spa
woo
son
lon

A
and
sma
has
oper
cros
hun
are
as
vess
they
sand

No
said
to a
and
rone
cerne
tinen
Alasl
with
moun
clima

* " A
† " A

eral volcanoes are found in the range. At present inactive, they are liable to burst forth at any time. These mountains, as a rule, are well clothed with trees and shrubbery. Practically every foot of space, both on the islands and the mainland, is wooded. Arms of the ocean indent the mainland, some of them being more than a hundred miles long.

Alaska is a country of magnificent distances, and no one thinks anything of travelling, even in small craft, several hundred miles. The writer has made trips of over four hundred miles in an open dory, carrying a tent, camping nights, and crossing large bodies of water. The natives travel hundreds of miles every year in their canoes. We are reliably informed that years ago they went as far south as San Francisco in these little vessels. It is a matter of undisputed fact that they frequently went for trade to Victoria, a thousand miles from the tribes farthest north.

CLIMATE

Notwithstanding all that has been written and said to the contrary, the impression still prevails to a large extent that Alaska is a bleak, barren and frigid country. Nothing could be more erroneous so far, at least, as the south coast is concerned. " Probably no other section of this continent presents such a diversity of climate as Alaska." * " In a country as extended as Alaska, with its large rolling plains, wide valleys and high mountains, there is necessarily a wide diversity of climate." † " As well might a person ask about

* "Alaska," Bruce, page 26.
† "Alaska," Jackson, page 52.

the climate of the United States without particularity, as to propound the same inquiry concerning Alaska." *

The climate of Alaska, like that of the United States, varies according to the locality and the season of the year. The section of the country occupied by the Thlingets seldom experiences the extremes of heat and cold. "Zero weather is a rare occurrence in Sitka, and there have been winters when the temperature seldom fell to the freezing point." "What is true of Sitka in this regard applies to all of southeastern Alaska."

The mean winter temperature of southeastern Alaska is about that of Washington, D. C. Navigation in this part of the country is open every day in the year. During the writer's long period of residence in Alaska, he has not seen a day when steamers could not land at the local wharves. This relative mildness of winter on the south coast of the territory is due in part, at least, to the warm Japanese (Kuro-Siwo) current which crosses the Pacific and splits on the Aleutian islands, one branch flowing north and the other south along the coast.

The summers in southeastern Alaska, the home of the Thlingets, are cool and moist. Nothing is more convincing as to the climate of Alaska than its vegetation. Great varieties of small fruits, such as strawberries, raspberries, huckleberries, cranberries, thimbleberries, salmonberries, currants, crabapples, and others are native to the soil, while all kinds of hardy vegetables are easily and abundantly cultivated there. A great variety of wild flowers, among them the daisy, dandelion,

* "Alaska: Its Resources, Climate and History," Swineford, page 91.

violet, rose and bluebell prove its temperate climate. The presence of butterflies, hummingbirds and robins also testifies that Alaska is not perennially frigid.

With less moisture, the summers of southeastern Alaska would be ideal. As it is, they are preferable to some of the hot regions of the States. The climate is neither so hot as to enervate nor so cold as to paralyze human efforts.

RESOURCES

The resources of a country, like the climate, have much to do with the habits and character of its people. In sunny climes, where breadstuffs grow without cultivation, and may be plucked any hour the inhabitant wishes to appease his hunger, we find a different character from that in the country where man has to wrest his living from the soil, the forest, or the water, by hard work and exposure.

While the resources of Alaska are varied and abundant, yet they are such as to demand of him who would obtain them industry, strength, endurance, courage and, in many instances, ingenuity.

" This is the law [of Alaska], and ever she makes it plain:
Send not your foolish and feeble; send me your strong and your sane."

The principal natural food resources of the Thlingets are fish, game and berries, and of these there is great variety.

Some kinds of fish and all berries may be had

only in their season, which is short. For winter consumption, these must be secured in their season, and properly cured and preserved. To this extent, at least, the people are provident. Venison and halibut may be had fresh the year round, yet they are also cured to some extent for winter use. Fish and seal oils are put up in summer, as well as delicacies, such as seaweed and herring.

The native of Alaska must not only hunt the game that he uses for food, thus requiring strength, labour and courage, but when he kills it he must dress and cook it before eating it. He must also provide fuel both to cook his food and to give him warmth.

Such requirements are not calculated to encourage indolence, and we find, as a rule, that the Thlinget is industrious, hardy and brave. He sails the deep in frail and cranky canoes, scours the forest for ferocious animals, and often meets his human antagonist without fear.

Of late years industries introduced by the white man have sprung up in this country which open new avenues of employment for the native. The mines, canneries, sawmills, fisheries, and other industries call for his brawn, if not his brain. Enlightenment is creating new and varied desires which impel him to greater exertion.

II

ABORIGINES OF ALASKA

A the present day there are not, all told, more than thirty thousand of the aboriginal stock in Alaska. These are scattered over the vast domain, no one locality being thickly populated. The native population has been slowly decreasing.

Excluding the minor tribes known as Hydahs and Tsimpsheans, the natives fall into four great divisions.

In their natural order, travelling north from Ketchikan, the first port of call, they are the Thlingets of Southern Alaska, the Tinneh of the Interior, the Aleuts of the southwestern panhandle, and the Eskimos inhabiting the shores of Bering Sea and the Arctic Ocean. These main divisions are again subdivided into tribes and families.

Different writers give different divisions of the natives of Alaska, some of these being not only incorrect but fanciful. " While there are twelve tribes, there are only two families, known as the ravens and eagles," seriously writes one author. Evidently the twelve tribes of Israel have given him a suggestion.

There are not only two but various families of each great division. " The Indians (Alaskans) are again subdivided into various families, each of which has its family badge," says Dr. Sheldon Jackson.

Mrs. Ella Higginson, in her work on Alaska, goes to the other extreme by making only two divisions of the natives—the Thlingets (or coast Indians) and the Tinnehs (or interior Indians), making the Thlingets to comprise the Tsimpsheans, Hydahs and Yakutats. But the Thlingets have a common language and the Tsimpsheans and Hydahs, who speak an entirely different language, should not be included with them. The Yakutats, on the other hand, speak the Thlinget tongue and should not be regarded as other than Thlingets.

This same writer, who seems to have a predilection for dual divisions, divides the Thlingets into two tribes, the Stikines and Sitkans. The Stikines and Sitkans are not tribes, but peoples of their respective localities, the same as those who live in Boston are Bostonians, whatever their nationality.

Tourist writers fall into many errors when they assume to write about the natives, as they cannot be comprehended at a glance nor their customs understood without months, if not years, of close observation.

Each division comprises people of a different type and language from all the others; each has its own specially well-defined territory and climate, and the customs of the people in one differ in many respects from those in the others. The territory of each division is widely separated from that of the others. The Thlingets are hundreds of miles from the Aleuts, Tinnehs and Eskimos. It is as rare to see an Eskimo or an Aleut in the land of the Thlingets as in Chicago, and an Eskimo is as much an object of curiosity to the Thlinget as to an inhabitant of Illinois. In over twenty

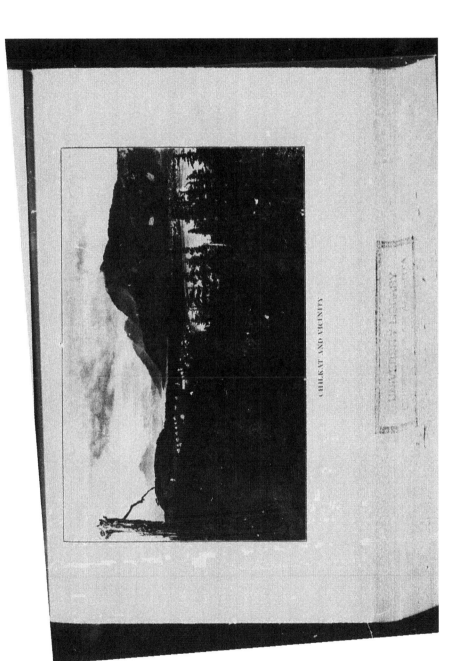

CHILKAT AND VICINITY

years of residence there the writer saw but three Eskimos, and these were witnesses in a suit.

The Thlingets occupy a score or more of villages in what is generally known as southeastern Alaska. The Tongass tribe embraces the natives in and around Tongass; the Hanega, those of Klawock and vicinity; the Stickeens, those at Wrangell; the Kaaks are in and near Kake; the Takoos and Anks are found at Juneau; the Sitkans at Sitka; the Yakutats at Yakutat, and the Chilkats at Haines and vicinity.

These communities are composed of different peoples. At Sitka we have the Kŏk-wŏn-tŏn', the Kăk-sŭ'dy and the Klŭk-nă-hŭ'dy tribes; at Hoonah the Dŭk-dain-tŏn' and the Chŭ-kă-nă'dy; at Haines (or Chilkat) the Kŏk-wŏn-tŏn', Klŭ-kă-hŭ'dy, and the Dŭk-lă-wă'dy; at Juneau the Nŭsh-kĕ-tŏn', the Auk and the Klĕ-nă'dy.

Where new communities have sprung up through the agency of the white man, such as Douglas, Skagway and Petersburg, the natives living in them are from various villages and tribes. They simply go to these places for employment. They may live in such places indefinitely, but they never regard them as their homes. Ask a native, " Where is your home? " and he will invariably name the village in which he was born.

Besides the divisions already mentioned, the tribes are subdivided into clans and families, with their distinctive totemic badges or crests and family house (Hit). These divisions will be further enumerated when we come to speak of totemism. The two great totemic divisions of the Thlingets are the *Yălkth* (Crow) and the *Tschäk* (Eagle).

The various tribes come under one or the other of these main divisions.

While the Thlingets from Tongass on the south to Chilkat on the north, a distance of over four hundred miles, are of the same stock and speak the same language, yet the enunciation is a little different in each community. One finds this an obstacle in using the language; if he learns it from the Chilkats and tries to speak it with the people of Wrangell he can scarcely make himself understood. Among the natives themselves, who are familiar with the different shades of enunciation, there is little or no difficulty.

Again, while these Thlingets are all of the same stock, some communities have been more progressive than others. The Chilkats were always a haughty and aggressive people. For years they held and controlled the trade with the interior, or Tinneh, Indians, and even disputed the right of the white man to advance through their boundaries to the land beyond. The Hootz-na-oos of Angoon (Killisnoo) were of a turbulent and warlike disposition for generations, and were only subdued by force of arms. The Auks (at Juneau) have always been regarded as a poor and spiritless class, and are more or less despised by the other natives.

They are all a maritime people, and their main food supplies come from the water. The canoe (yäk) or boat (ŏn-tă-yäk-oo') is to the Thlinget what the camel is to the Bedouin of the desert.

ORIGIN OF THE ALASKANS

WHENCE came the natives of Alaska? This subject has invited much speculation and many conjectures. In the absence of any recorded history concerning them, the question will probably never be positively determined. Some have come to one conclusion and some to another. The consensus of opinion, however, points to an Asiatic origin.

The theory that they are of Mexican origin has few to advocate it and very little to support it. It rests on the one fact that articles common to both have been found in Alaska. This proves nothing. The early Spanish explorers might have been the importers of these articles. Races wholly independent of each other have many things in common. The Hindoo of India has some things in common with the Mexican; and yet who would assert that the former sprang from the latter?

It is only natural that different people, though occupying the very antipodes of the globe, should hit upon some ideas and produce some things alike. Human needs, especially where people stand on the same plane of life, are very much the same.

The first implements of all untutored races would naturally be of stone· their first weapons, clubs, spears, bows and arrows; their clothing, skins and furs. So the possession of some things in common does not prove relationship.

The theory that the native of Alaska is an offspring of the North American Indian stands about on the same par with the Mexican.

Professor Dall, a man of exceptional ability, rather favours this view. He maintains, in one of his reports, that the natives of Alaska were once inhabitants of the interior of America, and that they were forced to the west and the north by tribes of Indians from the south. He makes the rather remarkable statement that he can in no way connect them with the Japanese or Chinese, either by dress, manner or language.

This is surprising, coming as it does from a man of his intelligence and research. Even tourists and transients passing through Alaska have observed the striking resemblance of native Alaskans to Japanese. The Thlingets, especially, seem so closely related to the people of the east coast of Asia, that a European traveller who had been around the world once remarked to a missionary, "How many Japanese you have in Wrangell!" At the time there was not a Japanese in the place. The people he saw were native Alaskans.

It is a common occurrence for these natives to be mistaken for Japanese. Some of them are facetiously called "Japs" by their own people. Minor W. Bruce, in "Alaska," says: "Prof. Otis T. Mason of the same institution [Smithsonian] takes the position that the emigration came from Asia to this continent, and that the Alaska Innuits are, undoubtedly, of Mongolian origin.

"We are also constrained to take this view,

and believe they once came across Bering Strait.
The same straight black hair, olive complexion,
small stature, almond-shaped eye and unusually
small hands and feet, are, to our mind, unmistaka-
ble evidence of kinship.

" They are not an inventive people, but are de-
cidedly and emphatically imitative, a trait in the
Japanese character always so conspicuous. And
their genius seems best illustrated in the nicety
of their carving."

The Hon. Wm. H. Seward says: " I have min-
gled freely with the multifarious population (of
Alaska), the Tongas, the Stickeens, the Kakes, the
Haidas, the Sitkas, the Kootnoos and the Chilkats,
but all of them are manifestly of Mongol origin.
All alike indulge the tastes, wear a physiognomy
and are imbued with sentiments peculiarly noticed
in China and Japan."

Charles Replogle, for many years a missionary
in Alaska, observes in his book, " Among the Indians of Alaska," " The origin of the native is
shrouded in the misty veil of the traditions of
their past. There is much reason to believe they
originally came from the continent of Asia. They
have the eyes of a Japanese, or very much the
same; the colour of their skin also resembles the
Jap."

The Hon. A. P. Swineford, once governor of
Alaska, writes: " Various theories speculative as
to their origin have been advanced. That those
of the coast and the islands as far north as to
where the Eskimos have their most southerly
habitation, are a distinct race, without a drop of
the blood of the American Indian in their veins,
unless it be in some instances of cross breeding,
is scarcely to be gainsaid.

" They are not Indians in the common acceptation of the term, but are, undoubtedly, of Asiatic origin. They are naturally bright and quick-witted people, with a Japanese cast of features."

The Rev. J. P. D. Llwyd, of Seattle, in his interesting little book, " The Message of an Indian Relic," says: " Students of ethnology are not yet agreed as to their origin, although the weight of argument seems to support the view that they are a branch of the Asiatic peoples, and are near of kin to the Japanese, whose cast of features is strikingly reproduced, for instance, in the children seen by travellers in the Indian village of Sitka."

We discover traits in the natives of Alaska found in the Mongolians. They are both skilled carvers in wood, and in carving they draw the knife toward the body instead of shoving it away in Yankee style. Both have a fondness for squatting on the floor and for eating from one dish in common; both have profound reverence for their ancestors, the Mongolians literally worshipping them. The Alaskans have a strong predilection in this direction, as their feasts for the dead evidence. Both quickly adapt themselves to the ways of progressive peoples. In this respect, the Alaskans are much superior to the Indians of the States. Centuries have elapsed since civilization was introduced to the latter, and yet many of them remain, practically speaking, savages. On the other hand, only a few years have elapsed since civilization, in any marked degree, was introduced to the former, and yet to-day we can find no savages among them, while many of them are fully enlightened.

The Alaskan's docility marks him as one who

has sprung from a different race than that of the wild, inflexible Indian of the Rocky Mountains. Then, too, the Alaskan is a maritine being, loving the sea as he loves his life. His home, if he is to be happy, must border on the same. Even the women are sailors. This trait corresponds with the sea-loving disposition of the Japs.

Another fact which lends strong support to the theory is that the Alaskan coast is directly opposite the shores of the Mongolian, and in one part, at least, not so very far away from them. This would afford an easy opportunity for any Japanese or Chinese adventurers to reach Alaska by design or accident. Columbus-like, some bold Asiatic adventurers may have landed upon the Alaskan shores, and from them may have sprung the new racial branch. Or, possibly, generations ago, some tempest-tossed Japanese or Chinese junk was driven upon our rugged Alaskan coast, and the occupants of this unfortunate craft formed the nucleus of the new race. Within recent years Asiatics have been stranded on these shores; and why not some centuries ago?

The Russians found in Kamchatka, before they discovered Alaska, Japanese writings and sailors. The Chukchi, the aborigines of Kamchatka, bore evidence of Mongolian origin. From this wing of the Asiatics might have come the Alaskans. In the summer time the trip from the country of the Chukchi to Alaska can be made in one day by canoe, and in the same time in winter by a swift reindeer team.

The aborigines of Kamchatka were continually trying to impress upon the minds of their Russian masters that the people in Alaska were like themselves. The early Russian historians bear wit-

ness to this: " In the other land [Alaska],"
writes one, " the people are like the Chukchi, without any government."

" Opposite the Cape [Noss]," writes another,
" lies an island [Diomedes] inhabited by people
resembling the Chukchi."

" The interpreters accompanying the expedi-
tion [Waxel's] belong to the Korick and the Chukchi tribes . . . being in outward appearance
like themselves [the natives of Shumagin]." *

" There are able students of ethnology who insist upon the origin of these Alaskans being Asiatic for various good and sufficient reasons,
instancing not only their personal resemblance,
but the similarity of their traditions and customs
to those of the people of Asia. To have come
thence it is remembered they had only to cross
a narrow piece of water forty miles wide. This
passage is frequently made in our time in open
boats."

But while the preponderance of facts is greatly
in favour of an Asiatic origin for the aborigines
of Alaska, there is still another view of the matter
that merits some consideration.

John W. Arctander, in " The Apostle of
Alaska," writes: " Where the Tsimpshean origi-
ally came from, it is impossible to ascertain.
Those who associate them, even in the distant
past, with the Japanese or the Koreans, certainly
do not find any very good arguments for their
contention. They perhaps drifted northward
long ago from some tropical island in the Pacific."

Mr. Arctander does not cite his reasons for
holding this view of the origin of the Tsimp-

* Bancroft.

sheans. He probably bases his opinion on the similarity of customs between the two people.

While it is true they have many customs and superstitions in common, yet this is no sure criterion by which to determine the origin of a people. It were just as reasonable to infer from such premises that the people of the islands in the Pacific sprang from the Alaskans.

The negroes in the dark jungles of Africa have many superstitions and customs in common with the natives of Alaska, yet who would be justified in declaring, because of this fact, that the Alaskans have sprung from the Africans? There is absolutely no relationship or connection between the two races.

There is scarcely a custom of the Alaskans that does not have its counterpart with the Islanders of the Pacific. The custom of secluding a girl when she becomes of age, of young girls marrying old men and young men marrying old women, of the father having no relation to his own children, of the property of the dead reverting to the opposite tribe of the deceased, of pregnant women observing taboos, of tattooing the body, of dancing and feasting, of pampering children, of shamanism and witchcraft, of the brother of a deceased brother taking his widow to wife, of gifts being passed to the parents of the bride, of weaving baskets, of marrying at an early age, of looking upon twins as an evil omen, of weaning children very late, and practically all the other customs of the Thlingets are followed by the inhabitants of the islands of the Pacific.

Then the two peoples are alike in personal appearance, temperament and traits. Both possess the happy and unhappy qualities of childhood, the affection, credulity, love of pleasure; also ungovernable passions, instinctive aversions, jealousy, cunning and a love of revenge.

We believe that both the Islanders and the Alaskans are of Mongolian origin, chiefly Japanese, and that the Alaskans were the first scion from this stock, and the Islanders, for the most part at least, indirectly of the same through the Alaskans. It is far more probable that the islands were first peopled from the mainland, rather than the mainland from the islands.

After studying the problem for years we believe the racial flow was along the Asiatic coast to Kamchatka, thence to Alaska, and from Alaska to the islands of the Pacific. This would account for the similarity of the many customs observed by the two peoples.

It may be asked, if the Alaskans have sprung from so happy a stock as the Japanese, why are they so much inferior to them? We reply, because generations, possibly centuries, of isolation have made them so. It is a well-known fact that degeneracy generally follows such a state.

Until a more plausible theory of the origin of our Alaskans is advanced, supported by stronger arguments than the foregoing, we shall continue to believe that our neighbour, Japan, is responsible for the existence of this aboriginal people.

IV

THE THLINGET LANGUAGE

AN interesting and instructive volume might be written on the language of the Thlingets, but only a chapter can here be given to it.

They have no written language. Their totemic emblems are the nearest approach to it.

Their oral language is handed down from generation to generation. It is constantly undergoing change, and already many terms once commonly used have become obsolete. Many of the natives now living have lost much of the pure Thlinget, and are unacquainted with many words which their ancestors employed. Then, again, new words are being coined to meet the growing demands superinduced by their progress in civilization.

It is especially interesting to note Thlinget word-building relative to objects introduced to them by white people. "Cream of Wheat" is called *säk-ă-hä'goo* because it resembles oolikan spawn. *Gŭn-teen'yäk* is the word for steamboat, which analyzed is *gŭn*(fire)-*teen*(with)-*yäk* (canoe), hence steamboat is canoe-with-fire. *On-tă-yäk-oo'*, the word for small boats other than canoes, little-canoe-on-ship—that is, lifeboat. These lifeboats were the first small boats other than their canoes that the natives ever saw, so *ŏn-tă-yäk-oo'* is the word used to differentiate all small boats from canoes. Ice cream is called *ā-ŭk-ă-hŭg'wă* (frozen grease); Epsom Salts, *kō-wän-nouk'*, frost medicine, because it resembles frost; *goolth'dān*, excitement, is derived from *goolth* (whirlpool). Lima beans are known as *wŭtzē-watze*, because they resemble the fat seen in the moose. " Quaker Oats " resembles the seed of the native wild celery (*yä-nă-āte'*) and for this reason is called *yä-nă-āte'shŭk-ā-hee'ny*.

Many white people, from some peculiarity, are nicknamed by them and these names become part of their vocabulary. One man is known as *Thloo'-tŭk-ăn* (red-inside-of-nose); another, *Ki-tik-kleak'* (one arm).

The language now abounds with corruptions through the effort of the natives to adopt or incorporate words from the English and Russian into their own tongue. Their word *dŏn'nă* is a mispronunciation of dollar, *Kin-ditch'* for King George, and *Kin-ditch-wän'* (King George's people) for Canadians. *Kin-ditch-wän-gŏt'ly* is the name of an island in the Chilkat river, so called because some Canadians once camped there. *Gŏw'ē* is a Thlinget corruption for the English coffee, and *goo-nāsh'es* for molasses. We might multiply examples almost indefinitely, but those cited will suffice for our purpose.

Some of their borrowed words which they have incorporated they pronounce correctly. Among these are sugar and butter in English, and *shă-deen'gă* (pig) and *wŏs* (cow) in Russian.

An invention known as the Chinook, a jargon, has also had a share in corrupting the pure Thlinget. Terms from this linguistic hybrid are frequently mixed with the Thlinget. Such terms as *Siwash* (Indian), *skookum* (strong), *tillicum*

(people), *tenas* (little) and many others are pure
Chinook words.

All Thlinget proper names have a meaning;
Shä-wät-klēn' (female) means big woman; *Kä-ŭk-
ish'* (male) means father-of-the-morning; *Shä-
goon-ē-ish'* (male) father-of-tools. All names applied to persons are in a sense inherited and
handed down from generation to generation.
While the Thlingets have no surnames, yet most
of them have more than one name. Some have
three or four. They need no surnames for iden-
tification, as the family crest serves this purpose.
Their names refer to this crest or totem, and as
soon as one hears the name of another he knows
exactly where to place him.

The name of a man is changed when he becomes a father and he is called after his child
with the word *ish* (father) appended. If, for instance, the child's name is Hŭlt-zoo', the father
is called Hŭlt-zoo-ish' (the-father-of-Hŭlt-zoo').

Certain proper names belong to certain tribes,
and only members of the tribe to which the names
belong can assume them. By this system each
name bears on the totem of the family, and the
individual is classified as soon as his name is
spoken. If he is among strangers, his name will
show who are his tribal relations. This secures
him friendship and hospitality.

Many of the natives now have full English and
Russian names in addition to their Thlinget
names. The writer himself has given English
names to more than seven hundred of them.

The paucity of the Thlinget language is not so
great as many white people are prone to think.
One thing is sure, the native is never at a loss
to express himself in his own tongue. This, how-

ever, may not be due so much to a lengthy vocabulary as to the gift of speech; the English is abundantly sufficient for expression, yet not a few English-speaking people find it difficult to express themselves.

Many Thlingets are eloquent in speech. Imagery is very largely used by them. A native youth in a speech likened the Presbyterian Training School to the Sitka harbour which is sheltered from the ocean waves by numerous islands—so the teachers stand round and about the pupils to protect them from the evils of the world.

The Thlinget language does lack, however, words to express abstract, spiritual and philosophical ideas. It contains no profane words nor any oaths. If the native wishes to swear, he must go outside of his own language to do it. But it abounds with vulgar and sarcastic terms, and these are freely employed when one wants to tongue-lash another.

What it lacks in abstract terms it makes up in the concrete. For example, where we make the one word "nephew" apply either to a sister's or a brother's son, the Thlingets employ different words. *Doo-hŭn-hä-yeet'* (nephew) is the older brother's son; *doo-keek-yeet'*, the younger brother's son, and *doo-kälth'k'*, the sister's son.

The same peculiarity obtains when they are speaking of brothers and sisters. The word differs according to whether one is speaking of an older or younger brother or sister, or whether a woman or a man is speaking. *A-hoon'* is the word used for brother when a younger brother is speaking of an older one; *ä-keek'* when a sister is speaking of her brother; *ä-shŭt'k'* when a younger sister is speaking of an older sister;

ä-keᴊk' when an older sister is speaking of a younger sister, and *ä-klòk'* when a man is speaking of his sister.

Sŭn'ny (uncle) is the word employed when speaking of one's father's brother, and *kŏk* (uncle) when speaking of a mother's brother. *Ot* (aunt) is used when speaking of a father's sister, and *klouk* (aunt) when speaking of a mother's sister.

Different terms are used for the same object according as to whether it is near or far off when you are speaking of it. Some things have three or four names.

But while the Thlinget language has more of a vocabulary than most people think, yet it is extremely deficient for the needs of this age. The paucity of the language may be better understood by giving an illustration. The best translation that can be made of our familiar doxology, and the one that is used in worship, is the following:

> " De-ke On-kow kuni-shag,
> Chuth-la-cut ha-jeg ya-a-ya-oo,
> Uch chuth-la-cut ye-wanch kuni-shag,
> Kuni-shag ha-ish tlahl-oohl-took."

This is the literal English translation:

> Above chief praise,
> All of us gifts,
> For all you praise,
> Praise our Father very pure.

Scarcely a sentence is spoken in which a peculiar and distressing guttural does not appear. This alone makes it very difficult for a white man to acquire. We have no alphabetical character to correspond with this guttural, and with some of us our vocal organs seem utterly incapable of producing it.

Although the Thlingets have no written language yet, the grammatical construction and sentence structure of their language are in form very much like the Latin. The verbs are similarly conjugated, the nouns similarly declined. There are but few of the former in the language, verb phrases being largely used instead, and these are conjugated as verbs. The personal pronoun is expressed wholly or in part, or implied, in every verb or verb phrase.

There is no verb " to be " in the language. *Yă-yă-tee'* (it abides) comes the nearest to it. There are no separate auxiliaries such as will, may, must, etc., as we find in English.

The verbs have Voice, Mood, Tense, Person and Number. The nouns and pronouns are declined in seven cases. The plural of some nouns is an entirely different word from the singular, corresponding in this respect with some of our English plurals. For instance *yŭd-ă-gwŭtz'koo* (boy) and *kă-sä'nee* (boys); *shŏt-gwŭtz'koo* (girl) and *shŏk-sä'nee* (girls).

As to gender, the word used determines whether the object is male, female or neuter. The feminine gender of animals is determined by the syllable shĕch; *goo-wă-kŏn'* (der) and *shĕch-goo-wă-kŏn'* (doe). Shĕch'-ä being the generic term for all female animals.

Like the Latin, the Thlinget language has no article, and, practically speaking, no preposition. *Kä* (and) is its main and almost its only conjunction.

In the structure of the sentence the usual order is (1) object, (2) subject, and (3) verb.

The Thlinget language is doomed to speedy extinction, the sooner the better, for the natives. They have no access to literature so long as they are shut up to their own language, and so they miss its elevating influences. In the second place, their language is useless as a means of communication with white people who are now populating their country and with whom they must now cope. It is certain that the white people will not learn Thlinget. If, therefore, the natives would do business with the white people, or be acquainted with the white man's laws by which they must be governed, they must learn English. In the third place, their language is altogether inadequate for their needs as their intellectual horizon widens. In the fourth place, the adoption of English means that they will far more rapidly get away from their old, degrading customs. Nothing retards the progress of a people so much as to be held to a language fit only for barbarians.

The sooner, therefore, that the natives drop their stunted and dwarfed language for the liberal English, the better. No encouragement to hold on to their language should be given by missionaries and teachers learning it with the view of addressing them in it. The best way of elevating them is to make them climb up to us.

While it was necessary for missionaries, teachers and traders to learn something of their language when they first went among them, it is not required now. Many, especially among the young people, have already a good command of English and some use English only. The day is not far distant when native audiences can be addressed directly in English without the medium of an interpreter. Then their complete civilization and progress to qualification for citizenship will be rapid.

Mr. William Duncan, who has so nobly, unselfishly and heroically laboured for more than fifty years with the Tsimpsheans of Alaska, declares his people are not yet qualified for citizenship. May it not be that holding on to their own tongue is largely responsible for this? Their language is useless outside of their own little community; why perpetuate it when they might have one that is universally used and the use of which would increase their knowledge a hundredfold and qualify them to take their places as citizens in the body politic?

It would be folly to attempt to reduce the Thlinget to writing and ask the natives to learn it. The time had better be spent in acquiring mastery of the English.

Were the Thlingets a great and flourishing nation like the Japanese or Chinese, or even multitudinous like the Africans, giving promise of indefinite perpetuation like these and similar people, then it would no doubt be wise to give them a literature in their own tongue as well as in a foreign one; for in these multitudinous races many will never know any other than their own language and the race is itself, relatively speaking, perpetual. But with the little tribes of Alaska it is very different. There is but a mere handful of any one of them, the white races are rapidly crowding them to the wall and nothing can stop it, there is little in their languages to merit perpetuation, and the sooner they acquire the pre-

vailing language of the land the better chance they
will have for existence and growth.

While in some localities, especially in the extreme southeastern part of the archipelago, the
Chinook jargon is used to some extent, in others
it is scarcely spoken at all. It was invented as a
means by which traders might communicate with
the natives of different tongues scattered along
the coast from Oregon to Yakutat, Alaska.

Very few of the natives living north of Wrangell have any acquaintance with it, and those who
have, seldom use it. It has little to recommend
it to the serious consideration of any one, other
than a curiosity. Its vocabulary is very limited,
it has no grammatical construction, and is not a
language, but an invention pure and simple. This
last fact is the only thing that makes it of any
interest.

V

THE FAMILY

THE husband and wife always belong to different tribes. According to a long-established custom, a Thlinget cannot marry one of his own totem, though no blood relation.

The children belong to the totem of their mother, and, of course, receive their caste from her. The father has no authority over his own children. The maternal uncle of the children has far more to say about them than the father. The aunts on the maternal side have, also, all authority over their nephews and nieces. They are regarded as mothers and are so called by their nephews and nieces. When the mother dies the father must relinquish his children to their maternal uncles and aunts. If the father were to inflict any injury on his child, his tribe would have to pay damages to his wife's tribe.

The father loves his children none the less because of this custom. He supports them to the best of his ability so long as they are under his care. When the mother dies and the children are taken by her relatives they assume their support. No child is ever cast out among the Thlingets. If a child loses both parents, some relation on the maternal side claims it and cares for it. Frequently disputes arise about who should have the orphan child, so desirous are relatives of taking their deceased relatives' children.

44

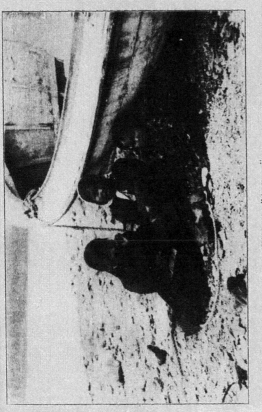

CHILDREN—"POSING"

t
e
g
li
u
n
in
w

pa
wl
so
for
fou
Th
wr
for
yea
F
girl
tha
C
mat
earl
afte
who
ther
stan
is th
mer
mout
were
as se
crime
bad l

The uncles and aunts are usually as good to their nephews and nieces as are their own parents—often better. Uncles are especially indulgent toward their nephews. In fact the more liberties they take the better the uncles like it. No uncle would think of imposing restrictions on his nephew in his own home, and the nephews walk in and out of the homes of their uncles as if they were real sons.

Children are very much desired by Thlinget parents. A barren wife is not enviable. Parents who are so unfortunate as to have no children sometimes adopt them. Such is their fondness for children that some natives have applied to foundling homes in Washington for white babies. The writer was asked by two native women to write to a foundling home in Seattle for children for them. Both have been married a number of years, but have no family.

Boys are, on the whole, more desirable than girls, because a man is esteemed of more worth than a woman.

Children born out of wedlock, especially illegitimate half-breeds, are more or less despised. In earlier times they were put to death immediately after birth. " Secret " children, that is, children whose fathers cannot be determined and who have, therefore, no visible fathers, are still in some instances destroyed as soon as born. Strangulation is the usual method of disposing of them. In former years they were taken to the woods, their mouths stuffed with moss or grass, and then they were thrown into a hole to die. This is all done as secretly as possible and to the natives it is no crime. They believe that if it is not done very bad luck will follow the family, or clan. It is a difficult matter to detect this crime, as they can go off to some unfrequented place, camp there for awhile, dispose of the new-born undesirable and when they return to town have a plausible statement to cover up the crime.

Until within recent years a regular doctor was never employed by the natives at childbirth and even now they are seldom called for such a purpose. The majority of Thlinget women suffer very little, and some not at all, when their children are born. They have been known to give birth while sleeping. In former years the universal practice was for the mother to lie outside of the house in a booth, or in the bushes. A hole was made in the ground and lined with leaves or moss and the new-born babe was deposited in it.

In an incredibly short time after giving birth to a child, the mother is up and about. They are often sitting up and sewing or doing bead or basket work in a few hours. " Delivery," writes Dall, " takes place in a few minutes, the mother kneeling; no pain is experienced, and she is about again and at her work in half an hour."

As soon as the Thlinget babe is born it is put into swaddling clothes and placed in a straitjacket like an Indian pappoose. It is practically kept in this for a year or more. Hammocks are made by doubling a blanket and running a rope through each fold. This is hung across one corner of the room and used as the cradle for the infant. A string is attached to one side of the hammock so that the mother, while at her sewing or basket-weaving, may pull it and keep the hammock in motion to rock the babe to sleep. Infants are seldom weaned under three years of age.

Children are so beloved by their parents that

they are indulged to their detriment. They are rarely punished. When they are it is because the parent has been grievously aggravated by them, and then punishment is brutally administered. The wishes of children are usually gratified to the extent of the parental ability. They are usually allowed to have their own way, and little or no parental restraint is thrown about them. This is due not so much to laxness as to misdirected parental love. It is considered a mark of their love to let their children have what they demand and do as they please.

Polyandry is rarely practised. In the many years of our residence among them, but two cases were reported to us, and those were not proven.

The domestic life of the average Thlinget family is of a low character. Most of the houses have but one room and no second story. In this one room several fam'lies frequently live a. the same time, eac' amily having its own personal effects, such as ling, cooking utensils, boxes of foo:, etc. Th. .oom is usually bare and scant of furniture, a box-stove being the most prominent piece. In some may be found bedsteads, either crudely made by the native himself or purchased, but the floor is oftener used for sleeping purposes. The bedstead often holds boxes, trunks and other articles.

Few homes have chairs, and those that have are not supplied with enough to go round. It is popular with the women to squat on the floor. While some households are furnished with a common table (often home-made), many families do not deem this an indispensable article of housekeeping. The meal is more frequently spread on the floor near the stove than on the table. No table-

cloth is used. Even where a home may have one
or more tables, there may be more families than
tables, and so some must take the floor. The general use of the table is to hold accumulated dirty
dishes. There is no regular hour for eating, and
any one is at liberty to cook at any moment of the
day or night. Husbands cook for themselves
nearly as often as their wives cook for them. If
the husband is hungry and wants his meal, the
wife gets it or not, as she is disposed.

The greatest disorder prevails in the average
home. We could hardly expect anything else
where several families live in one room, and each
wait for the others to clean up. Then, too, families are going and coming all the time, and we
hear them complain that they cannot keep a home
very clean for these reasons. The beds are mussy
and seldom made up. During the day they are
lounged on and slept in without the one using
them taking off any clothes. The Thlinget sleeps
whenever he is inclined so to do. We have found
them in bed at all hours of the day, and often seen
them sleeping with their clothes on as they came
off the street.

The dishes and skillets are usually dirty. Each
family cooks and eats at a different time from the
others in the house, and if all are using dishes and
skillets in common, those who use them last leave
them dirty for the next set to clean—if they wish
them cleaned. Often they use them as they find
them, dirt and all.

The popular method of cooking is boiling, although broiling and roasting are also used. In
former years, before they became acquainted with
the iron pot, they did their boiling in baskets
woven of the spruce fibre, and so closely as to be

water-tight. Stones were heated and dropped
into the contents of the basket and in this way
boiling was done. Few natives know anything of
pastry cooking.

Any member of the household eats and sleeps
and gets up when he feels like it. No restrictions
are imposed. They run in and out, engage in any
employment they please, all without let or hin-
drance. Some are packing up to move out while
others are moving in to stay.

Many of them own no home personally, but
move about from house to house among the tribe.
They are never at a loss to find some place in
which to stay, and that without cost. If the
owner is not at home any of his tribe may go in
and make themselves at home, and stay as long
as they please.

When they move they take all of their personal
effects with them, including the dogs.

Dogs are highly prized for hunting. Some men
own four or five. They are of a wolfish nature
and extremely mean. They are not regarded as
pets and are seldom treated as such. They are
left to get their own food. The natives have a
superstition about killing a dog. If some one else
kills him the owner appraises the dog very highly
and clamours for pay. He suddenly becomes a
valuable creature, though before he was killed he
was utterly worthless.

Clothes are washed in several ways. A common
method is to take them to a near-by stream, or
the bay, and wash them there by rubbing the garments between the hands or on a washboard.
Tubs are used in the house, but are invariably
set on the floor, the woman squatting beside them
while she rubs the articles on a washboard or

between her hands. Blankets are commonly washed by throwing them in the bay and treading on them. We have seen the women treading blankets when the weather was so cold that their feet and legs would be as red as beets.

Sewing is one of the domestic arts of the Thlingets. Not only do the women make garments and patch clothes, but they use the needle in making moccasins, mittens and various kinds of beadwork. Some of them handle the needle with much skill and do very fine work. In this age both hand and pedal sewing-machines are commonly used by them.

In the home life many things that we would regard as immodest cause no comment among the natives. A mother has no hesitancy in suckling her child in public, or men in lounging around half-clothed, or children in going practically nude.

Gossiping is one of the besetting sins of the women. You can hardly go into a home without encountering a group of gossips, and quarrels frequently result from rumours thus set in motion.

Family quarrels are all too frequent. Jealousy prompts some, while indiscreet acts and ungovernable tempers are at the bottom of others. The husband chastises his wife, sometimes beating her unmercifully. The wife does not always tamely submit to this, but defends herself to the best of her ability. Often she is more than a match for her husband in brute strength and in the science of handling her fists. Biting is a common mode of inflicting injury upon one another when quarrelling.

The status of a Thlinget wife is not that of a slave to her master. She is as independent as he, and she asserts her independence, too. In truth,

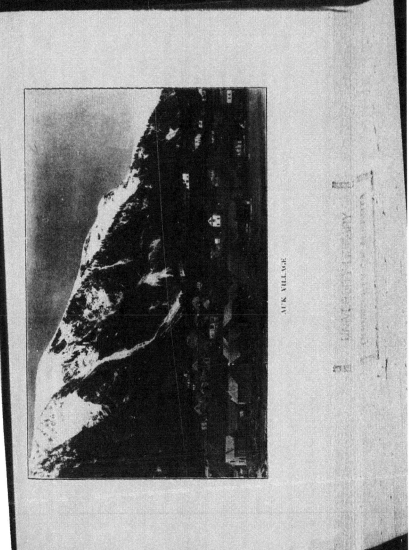

AUK VILLAGE

th
w
in
th
si
an
giv
ma
an
her
hov
cisi
stor
her
and
and
pen
and
whe
son
wom
woul
admi
did s
woul
spise

Sor
to th
reaso
of be
more
some

In t
as a v
in thi
slaver

the average husband stands more in fear of his
wife than she does of him. The husband's earnings are wholly turned over to his wife. She is,
therefore, the banker of the household. If he desires to make a purchase he must appeal to her
and get her consent. Sometimes she declines to
give him what he asks for, or disapproves of him
making the contemplated purchase. If spirited
and he realizes that he can master her, he forces
her to give him the required amount. Ordinarily,
however, he meekly acquiesces in the wife's de-
cision. If he wishes to buy any article in the
store, or from any one, she must first see it for
herself or be told about it. If she approves, well
and good. If she objects, that usually settles it
and the purchase is not made. She is so independent that she makes him wash his own clothes
and cook his own food. This is always the case
when she is angry at him for any cause. No person is more stubborn than the average Thlinget
woman. You can neither coax nor drive her. She
would sooner be beaten to a pulp than have to
admit she was compelled to do a thing. If she
did she would be sneered at as a slave, and that
would be worse than death, for slaves are despised as the very lowest of creatures.

Some consider it a mark of weakness to yield
to the demands of their husbands, and for this
reason they often oppose them. In fact, instead
of being drudges of their husbands, they do no
more than they feel disposed to do; and with
some this is very little.

In the Thlinget household there is no such thing
as a voluntary servant, or servant for hire; nor,
in this day, from compulsion. In the days of
slavery slaves were compelled to labour for their

masters and for their master's household. But
the days of slavery have passed.

The average Thlinget home is run in a loose,
slipshod fashion, but there are some which are
nicely kept, in which order prevails, where the
children are reasonably cared for, and where
marks of refinement are not wanting. In communities where the white population is considerable, native families live interspersed among them.
These families, as a rule, live along the advanced
lines of civilization and manage their homes as
creditably as the ordinary white families manage
theirs.

In taking native family life into account, it
should be remembered from what the people have
emerged, the many drawbacks with which they
have to contend, the little means and few facilities
they have at their disposal, and their lack of education. It is a question if the average white
woman placed in the same environment and under
the same handicaps would do any better than the
average Thlinget woman does in the way of keeping a neat and orderly home. The home lacks
every facility for good housekeeping, has but the
one room, without closets or racks for garments,
is subject to constant inroads of entire families,
and the housekeeper labours under conditions that
afford only a bare subsistence. All things considered, the Thlingets have made splendid progress. History shows that they have climbed away
from savagery much more rapidly than our savage
forefathers did, and much more rapidly than have
many other races.

VI

THE COMMUNITY

EACH community of natives is independent of every other. There is no federation. The only bond of unity is the tribal, or totemic, bond.

As a rule, the communities are many miles apart. Safe and cozy harbours, with nice beaches, are chosen for town-sites. "The native hamlets are always built near the shore, accessibility to the water being the first consideration, because from that source comes nine-tenths of their subsistence." *

The villages are constructed to conform to the contour of the shore. There is no such thing as laying out a town-site. They have no knowledge of surveying. The villages can hardly be said to have any streets, as every native is desirous of having his home directly on the water-front. But in most instances the beaches are short, between precipitous shore lines, so that some must build back from the shore.

By building next to the beach no clearing the ground is necessary. The Thlinget avoids all exertion possible; he will not cut down trees and dig out stumps for a clearing unless it is absolutely required. He usually claims no more ground than his house occupies, except the frontage. He has no homestead, nor ranch, nor estate. He can ac-

* "Alaska," Ballou, page 194.

53

quire no title to anything: land, homestead, mineral claim or any other property. It is hard to define the native's status. He is declared not a citizen of any country. Since he supports himself he is not a ward of any country. And yet the United States claims to have jurisdiction over him. It sues him and imprisons him, but it will not let him vote, have any voice in making the laws by which he is governed, or acquire title to property. In rights, he is treated as a foreigner, but in punishment as a citizen. If he has a house and land he cannot sell them and give title. Because of this anomalous position in which he finds himself, he has no incentive to acquire land and improve it, or to prospect for minerals. In but few instances has he profited from gold discoveries. Consequently all ambition in this direction is stifled. He plants his little home by the sea, or on the river bank, and therewith rests content.

Many of the houses are set at every conceivable angle. Had the houses in some villages been dumped out of the clouds they could scarcely have lodged in a more disorderly arrangement.

A monotonous appearance characterizes nearly every village. But still the people are improving in their building and give promise of approaching, at least, the ordinary home and architecture of the white man in the near future.

Years ago, while massive communal houses constituted some villages, others were composed of mere shacks and huts. The roofs were made of slabs and cedar bark carelessly thrown over pole rafters. No house had a chimney or a window. A large aperture in the centre of the roof served for both. They were put up in the most slipshod fashion, with the least labour possible, and had the appearance of being ready to tumble down.

In justice to the natives, be it said that they were not to blame for the squalid, miserable villages of years ago. In the first place, there are few places in southeastern Alaska suitable for a town-site, because the shores are so mountainous. In those days there were no sawmills, and every stick put into a house had to be hand-hewed. Then the few tools they had were very rude and they knew almost nothing about carpentry. Hence they were greatly handicapped and built under serious disadvantages.

Now they are in possession of good tools, have sawmills and hardware stores to draw on for suitable materials to put into buildings. They have also some knowledge of carpentry. Some have served apprenticeships to the trade and are now skilful in handling tools. These advantages have brought great changes in their building. The rude, dilapidated, windowless huts and hovels have been replaced with frame houses having windows and chimneys and shingled roofs. And not only have their homes been improved in outward appearance, but the interiors are incomparably better. Formerly they were never ceiled. The mere rough boards stared one in the face, with cracks wide enough to thrust the finger through them. But now their houses are ceiled and many of them nicely papered and painted. The new villages that have sprung up consist of up-to-date houses. There are several old, abandoned villages with ancient communal houses and totem poles. These primitive towns present a weird appearance, and, if they could talk, would tell some thrilling tales.

Changed conditions and the example of the
white people of the States have, no doubt, led to
these improvements. Under the Russian régime
the natives saw no modern style buildings.

In addition to the main villages, there are summer camps for fishing and berry picking, and
winter lodges for trapping and hunting. The territory of each community, that is, the fishing and
hunting territory, is well known to all. There is
no encroaching on one another's grounds, as all
are at liberty to roam where they will.

In every community there are two or more different tribes. A chief is at the head of each, and
nothing of importance is undertaken without first
consulting him. Generally his word is law with
his people. The individual counts for little unless
of high rank, or caste. The tribe is the ruling
power in every community, and usually does as
the chief says. All grievances are redressed and
reprisals made by the tribe. When an individual
is wronged the tribe at once takes up his cause;
when shamed or insulted, the tribe at once re-
sents it; when in need of assistance, the tribe is
ever ready to help him. Marriages, house building, burials, feasts, potlatches, dances, the erection of totem poles, and many other things are
matters for tribal consideration.

They have no municipal government nor public
utilities. There are no taxes, as there are no
public expenses or offices. The only public spirit
expressed is that through the tribe to its own
members.

As a community, they will suffer the greatest
inconvenience rather than lift a hand for the
public good. No one would think of removing the
carcass of a dead dog, or a salmon, from their

midst, of digging a well, or performing other
service for the public weal.

Not until recently have they shown disposition
to establish any public utilities whatever. Some
villages now have plank sidewalks and public
halls, and in one or two places they run a few
electric street lamps. In time the spirit may
grow.

In one community, that of Kluckwan, they have
installed a public water system, leading the water
from the mountain to the village through pipes.
The missionary of that place was the prime
mover in the enterprise. The natives rallied to
the rroject, and now they have good water with
strong pressure.

The sanitary conditions of nearly every native
community are deplorable. Were it not that the
beneficent tides flush the beaches twice every
twenty-four hours nothing could have saved them
from extinction years ago by some malignant epidemic produced by their own filth and carelessness.

In some localities, the more progressive and
enlightened natives live apart from the unsavoury
village. A number of native homes are known to
us that are as tidy and inviting as the ordinary
white man's home. At Sitka they have a cottage
settlement in connection with the Presbyterian
mission, which is a mile away from the common
native village. The cottages in this settlement
are occupied and owned by those who were once
pupils of the mission, but are now married and
have families. The homes are neatly furnished
and kept, and life is on a much higher plane than
in the ordinary native village.

The social life of the average native community

is of a very low tone. They have very little to
break the monotony of life. Aside from feasting
and dancing they have practically no amusements.
Public quarrels are common and a source of enter-
tainment to the staring spectators, as they rarely
fail to draw an audience. All domestic troubles
are fully aired and made subjects of gossip. Nothing is hidden, hence we see the entire dark side
of the native as well as his good side. They are
not as clever in this respect as the white people
are. There are no skeletons tucked away in native families, for the acts of one are familiar to
all the others. Privacy is hardly known among
them. It cannot be maintained very well under
their system of living, with families bunched together.

The Thlinget's bump of curiosity is well devel-
oped, and anything out of the ordinary, as an
accident, a birth, a death or a quarrel, never fails
to draw a crowd.

The women gossip unrestrainedly about every
one who comes to mind, and often mix their gossip
with many grains of falsehood. Some of them
have great ingenuity as fabricators, telling things
for fact that are a mere tissue of lies.

They walk in and out of one another's homes
without the formality of knocking on the door.
A woman may be in the very act of changing her
garments when Mr. Quakish steps in unan-
nounced to visit her husband. This does not em-
barrass her in the least. She proceeds as if no
one had called. They walk out as unceremoni-
ously as they walk in. Having sat long enough
they arise and walk out without saying a word
or taking notice of any one. In turn, the guest is
as little noticed. If the occupants of the house

are busy with sewing, making baskets, carving, etc., they never suspend work for a visitor. The men are very taciturn when visiting, often coming in and sitting for awhile without saying a word and then passing out.

Life in the village is very different in the summer from what it is in the winter. In the summer very few remain, some villages being absolutely deserted. The people are mostly off to their summer camps and places of occupation, hence it is very quiet in town. In the fall they return for the winter, and festivities begin. Winter is the Thlinget's play time. Summer is the time for work.

Rank and caste play an important part in every Thlinget community. While caste does not bear as vigorously on the Alaskans as it does on the Hindoos of India, yet it is very pronounced and severely felt.

There are four strata of Thlinget society, the high, medium, low and the slaves. There are none of the last now, except a few " left-overs." They all mingle in the community, the low and the high visiting and talking with one another. But in marriage, at feasts, in public councils, and in the settlement of wrongs and injuries, class distinctions are always asserted. The high-caste family strenuously opposes the marriage of one of its number to one of a lower class.

The sister of a certain chief known to us married one of a lower caste. The chief not only disowned her, but threatened to kill her for the disgrace. In earlier times a brother had the right to kill a sister who disgraced the family in any way.

A low-caste man paid the dowry for a high-caste woman. Her tribe quickly had it returned, as they would not countenance such a marriage.

At feasts they are given positions and goods according to rank and caste. In public councils it would be considered a shame for those of high-caste connections to listen to talk from those of a lower class. I once employed as church interpreter a native who had been a slave. The people of the higher classes refused to take instruction through such a medium. When I found out the reason of their coldness I changed interpreters, and the work took on new life from that moment.

The lines of caste are also marked by the attitude the lower take toward the higher classes. The low-caste man must be very careful what he says to the high-caste fellow. The man of high-caste totem can say what he pleases to a member of his own phratry who is of a lower caste, and the latter must meekly take it.

Caste is revealed in property affairs. The low caste are not allowed to erect houses and totems, or to build canoes equal to those of a higher class. Certain names are not allowed to be used by inferior classes. The totem governs all naming of the natives.

Tradition says that long ago the natives were savages and went naked. After awhile they made clothing of skins, and used sinews of animals for threads. The babies that were well cared for and wrapped in furs were considered superior to those that were wrapped in moss and neglected. The high-caste, or well-raised baby, had eight feasts given in its honour, and was then given an honourable name. Thus caste was established.

Children of high-caste parentage are high caste by inheritance. The child of parents who are high

on one side and low on the other loses caste. Men
of wealth, that is, those possessing many blankets,
trunks, and dancing paraphernalia such as masks,
hats, dancing robes, etc., are very highly esteemed. So are mighty hunters.

As caste serves to distinguish classes, rank does
the same for individuals. The Ikt (shaman) was
at one time the most highly revered person among
them. He was esteemed as one having supernatural powers, and was honoured above all
others not only in life but in death.

Next to the shaman in station is the chief (*ŏn-
kŏw'wă*). The office is hereditary or elective.
When the chief dies the office does not entail on
his son, as the crown does in European kingdoms,
but on his brother or his nephew, the son of his
sister—the son of the oldest if he has more than
one. This is to keep the chieftainship within the
correct tribal bounds. The man's son is never
a member of his tribe, but always of the mother's.
A man's sister's son is by force of custom always
a member of his clan or tribe. His brother's son
would not be. For this reason the son of the
chief's sister is recognized as the true heir to the
office of chief.

The chief is not only respected by all classes in
his community, but throughout the entire country,
no one daring to give him umbrage except one of
his own class or rank. He is generally obeyed and
supported by the members of his tribe. He con-
siders it beneath his dignity to carry the slightest
parcel. His game is procured and his domestic
fires are kept up for him. In former years, when
slavery was in vogue, his slaves did his bidding.
While his authority is not so great now as it was,
yet he has no trouble to find those who are obedi-

ent to his orders. He is respected at all feasts and potlatches, his being the seat of honour and the largest share in the distribution of goods. None of a lower rank is allowed to build so large a house as his, or give a greater potlatch. When one of his own tribe wishes to build, he dictates the dimensions of the house.

Some tribes have more than one chief. When this is so they are not of equal rank. The Thlingets are very supercilious about caste and rank. This does not appear on the surface, but is seen when we understand their customs.

In this day, we find in every considerable community two classes, the older ones, who are tenacious of the old customs and superstitions, and the younger ones, or rising generation, who are striving to get away from them. These two classes often conflict, but the former have mostly proven the stronger. Their power, however, is constantly waning and it is only a question of a few years when they and their customs will have gone forever. Some have entirely dropped the old customs and are living on the plane of the white man.

As the native communities in Alaska are constantly undergoing change, what is true of them to-day may not be true of them five or ten years hence. Many things that were true of them twenty years ago are not true of them now.

It would not be correct nor just to take descriptions of native communities written more than a score of years ago, as applying in all respects to the same to-day. Not only the houses, but many of the customs and manners which were common at that time have passed away. New conditions are constantly confronting the natives and they are more or less conforming to them. War, slavery, gambling, cremations, polygamy and other customs that were rife a generation ago are no longer practised.

Many communities are now populated by white people and natives. In some of these towns the natives live in a community by themselves, in others they are mixed in with the white races.

The founding of towns by white men has drawn colonies of natives from their own villages of ancient standing to such communities for employment, and this has had a marked effect on native life; in some respects for good and in some for evil. There are also two prominent factors in every village that were not to be found a little more than a generation ago—the church and the school.

VII

PERSONAL APPEARANCE, DRESS AND ORNAMENTATION

WHILE some of the natives take no pride in their personal appearance, many of them dress in good taste and make a very favourable impression. This is especially true of the rising generation, and may be taken as a mark of their progress.

The native youth wear good suits with up-to-date neckwear, and the young women have dresses and cloaks in harmony with the fashion of the day.

At home and in their own villages they are inclined to show an utter disregard of their personal appearance. The women are worse than the men in this respect. They not only go about their homes, but visiting through the village, with dishevelled hair and unlaced shoes. When they appear on the streets and in the stores of the white man's settlement they are dressed neatly and tidily, as a rule.

The men generally appear well in public, buying and wearing, for the most part, the best clothes that can be bought. This is especially true of those natives who live near any considerable white population.

The native dress is far in advance of what it was some years ago. For a long time the blanket was the principal, and often the only, article of dress.

Even to this day it is the only cloak used by some,
but as an article of dress it is practically a back
number.

We note again the evolution in the headgear of
native women. A few years ago the universal
headgear was a large kerchief. All kinds of
colours and combinations of colours were worn.
" Groups of natives in bright-coloured blankets,
with scarlet and yellow handkerchiefs on their
heads, come into view, watching us curiously
as we glide over the smooth water." * This
style of headgear has given way to hats and
bonnets.

Many have extra good clothing which they wear
only on special occasions, such as Fourth of July,
Christmas and Easter. At these times their
finery is brought out and worn for the day, then
taken off and laid away until the special day
comes round again.

Some display remarkably good taste and are
well and becomingly dressed, while others, having
no sense of the fitness of things, exhibit very bad
taste. An old woman will appear in dress and
colours suitable only for a girl, while a girl may
appear in such as are suitable only for elderly
persons. Their combinations of colours may do
all violence to good taste.

We must remember, however, that good taste is
the result of cultivation and education. Refined
taste is acquired, not inherited. Let a prince grow
up in a hovel from infancy and he may be coarse
and vulgar. On the other hand, put the child of
a beggar into a family of refinement and he is
likely to become refined in his manners and
tastes.

* Ballou, page 194.

So if we see our natives blundering in taste as they advance in civilization we should not be surprised nor ridicule them. It would be a marvel if they did not. It is really remarkable that so many of them appear in public so well dressed when we remember that the race has only recently had opportunities for development along these lines.

Their love of ornamentation is innate, but they are not peculiar in this. The farther down the scale of civilization the more pronounced is this characteristic, and it is carried in some instances to a ludicrous excess.

The Thlingets of to-day are not so given to personal ornamentation as they were a few years ago. Their taste in this respect, as in others, is constantly improving. Formerly their decorations were excessive, ludicrous and grotesque. Rings were worn not only on the fingers but in the ears and the nose. The cartilage in the nose of every Thlinget is punctured for nose rings, but these were worn only in dancing. Earrings are yet commonly worn by females. They were worn by men a few years ago, but now you rarely see one with them. At dances men, women and children wear them. Some men have three punctures for rings in each ear, one in the lobe, one in the middle, and one at the top. There are ear-drops made from shark's teeth that are highly prized. They are triangular in shape, and are worn only at dances. The upper end is usually mounted with gold or silver.

Every Thlinget child has his ears and nose pierced for rings the day he is born. Yarn or grass is put in the opening to keep it from growing together. In earlier years rings were worn in

the ears and nose, not only for ornamentation,
but to show that the child's parents were not
poor. If a child had no ring or jewellery of any
kind he was looked down upon and his people were
despised.

In early times earrings were made of copper,
silver and gold, and in shape were round, ex-
cepting the shark tooth pendant. To-day the style
of earring or pendant varies, as they have a wide
range from which to select.

The women and girls are very fond of the
finger-ring (*tlaka-keas*) and the bracelet (*keas*).
Even to this day women may be seen with rings
on every finger of each hand and several bracelets
on each wrist. These are made by native silversmiths out of silver and gold coin. The coin is
melted and pounded into shape and then all kinds
of totemic designs are carved on them. Some of
the bracelets are more than an inch wide, and
made not only of silver but of pure gold. The
latter range in value from twenty to forty dollars
each.

Until recently they preferred silver jewellery to
gold. Now that they know the value of gold, they
esteem the gold jewellery more highly.

Neck chains and stick-pins are commonly worn.
Formerly necklaces were made of shark's teeth,
shells, pretty beads and stones. While bead necklaces are still worn, they are being gradually supplanted by gold ones. Both gold and silver pins
are made in all kinds of designs (chiefly totemic)
by native silversmiths. Coin is invariably used
by native artists for all jewellery.

The ordinary native is as well satisfied with a
brass pin studded with glass gems as with one
of pure gold studded with diamonds. The glitter

is the chief consideration. But the better educated and more refined will not wear tawdry jewellery.

Their rings and bracelets are worn at all times; they never lay them off for drudgery or dirty work, not even when they go about with bare legs and feet.

The *labret* is a piece of bone or silver varying in size according to the rank of the person wearing it, that is inserted into the lower lip just below the mouth. It is worn as a sign of womanhood. Some assert that its original object was to keep women from talking, and that if a woman, while scolding, dropped her labret from her lip, she was considered beaten and disgraced. We have asked not a few natives if this be true, and all we have consulted have repudiated the story and insisted that it is worn as a badge of womanhood.

Only women of high caste are allowed to wear it. Slaves were strictly forbidden its use. As the woman who wears the labret grows older, its size is increased, so that a woman's age may be known from the size and kind of labret she wears. In some old women they are an inch long and a quarter of an inch wide. They certainly do not enhance a woman's looks, but on the contrary give her a hideous appearance.

" The author," writes Ballou, " has seen all sorts of rude decorations employed by savage races, but never one which seemed quite so ridiculous or so deforming as the plug (*labret*) which many of these women of Alaska wear thrust through their lower lips. The plug causes them to drool incessantly through the artificial aperture, though it is partially stopped by a piece of bone, ivory, or wood, formed like a large cuff-button, with a flat-spread portion inside to keep it in position. This practice is commenced in youth, the plug being increased in size as the wearer advances in age, so that when she becomes aged her lower lip is shockingly deformed."

It is only just to state that this custom, so far as the Thlingets are concerned, is a thing of the past.

Tattooing on some portions of the body was once a very common form of adornment, but is seldom, if at all, resorted to in this age. Only high-caste natives were permitted to have their bodies tattooed. Professional tattooers were employed to do this, and were paid large sums for their work. A feast was invariably given in honour of the occasion, which exalted the one tattooed in the public esteem.

Streaking the face with paint was another way they had of adorning the person—a custom no longer practised except for dancing. When this was done the tribal mark of the individual had to be used. For instance, a member of the Whale-killer (Keet) tribe wore a mark down the cheek and one at right angles to this across the chin. This marking represented the jaw of the Keet (grampus), and showed to the public that the one thus marked was of the Keet tribe. A member of the Crow (Yalkth) tribe had a line drawn on each side of the nose beginning at the inner corner of the eye and angling down the cheek. This represented the beak of the crow.

Even now many of the women paint their faces solidly with a kind of lampblack made of soot and grease. This is done, however, not for ornamentation, as it makes them hideous-looking in the ex-

treme, but for the double purpose of protecting
their faces from mosquitoes and sunburn.

In former years their dress was gorgeously
adorned with beads, buttons and abalone. At one
time the abalone shell was to the natives what
diamonds are to the white people. Many carvings
were inlaid with it. To this day it is highly
prized, and used for ornamentation. In the days
of slavery slaves were traded for it.

Dancing blankets and cloaks are elaborately ornamented with buttons and beads, making some
of them very expensive. Beads are commonly
used to ornament moccasins, pouches and wall
pockets that are made from deer and moose hide.
The beautiful green found on the head of the
mallard drake is very commonly used for adorning articles. The head is skinned and the entire
patch of green kept intact.

Our white sisters cannot criticise them for this
since they are so fond of adorning their own bonnets with the plumage of birds. Native women
do not use the mallard plumage for adorning hats
or bonnets, but for the decoration of pouches and
wall-pockets.

Most of the natives are slow of movement and
lacking in grace, but some have fine form and
carriage. Some of the young women are exceedingly attractive.

With them, as with white people, we find the
attractive and the repulsive, the neat and the tidy,
the respectable and the vulgar, the clean and the
filthy.

The Thlinget's standard of beauty is very different from that of the white man. Men whom
we would consider extremely ugly are very much
admired by Thlinget women. The large mouth,

thick lips and coarse features appeal to the average native. It would seem that the more hideous the face the more it is admired by the average Thlinget. The natural, soft, subdued olive complexion of the average Thlinget young woman is very pleasing.

The half-breeds are invariably bright and good-looking. Some of them are really handsome. They dress in good taste and present a good appearance. They are inclined to affiliate more with the white people than with the natives. It seems, indeed, to be their natural place and it is so accepted. They seek education and many of them after schooling drop into good positions among the white people. Some of them have shown high ability and are now in positions of responsibility. Possessing, as a rule, a captivating personality, they seemingly have but little trouble to find a place in the world.

VIII

INDUSTRIES

THE Thlingets, as already said, are self-supporting, not wards of the government. In fact they have been woefully neglected by the government. They ask only the opportunity to earn a livelihood and that their natural resources be not destroyed.

"Unlike the American Indians," writes the Hon. A. P. Swineford, at one time Governor of Alaska, "these people are industrious and self-supporting." Professor Dall bears testimony to the same truth.

Unfortunately for them, their industries are very limited and their seasons very short. Their main dependence is on fishing and employment in the canneries. They catch salmon and halibut for the local markets, shippers, salteries and canneries.

The halibut are caught with line and hook, herring being used for bait. The old style of hook was a V-shaped piece of wood with an iron tooth about two inches long projecting from the upper side almost across the angle of the hook, and pointing downward. The unwary halibut runs his nose into the V for the bait and becomes hooked. While some natives prefer this, most of them use the modern, up-to-date hook. The old style are sold as curiosities.

Formerly the halibut line, as was all rope, was

TREADWELL GOLD MINE

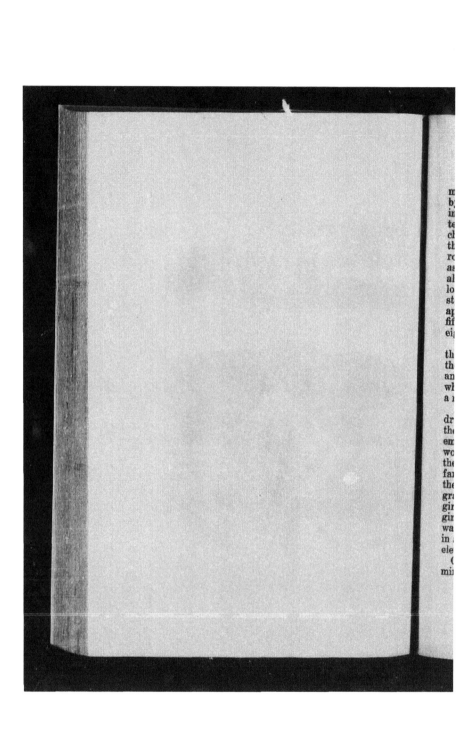

made of the fibre of the spruce tree and entirely
by hand. The women made it and became expert
in manufacturing cordage of all sizes. It was a
tedious job, and particularly wearisome to the
children who were compelled to hold one end of
the line while the mother wove the material into
rope. The lines were made many fathoms long,
as uniform as if made by machine, and exception-
ally strong. We have in our possession a very
long, native-made halibut line with hook (old
style) attached. It is a fine piece of work, and
apparently as strong now as when it was made
fifty years ago. It is doubled strand and three-
eighths of an inch in diameter.

The natives do not build fish-traps. A few of
them use gill-nets. By their methods of fishing
they could never destroy, nor even diminish to
any appreciable extent, the fish supply. It is the
white man with his seines and fish-traps that is
a menace to this natural resource of the country.

Not only the native men, but women and children, work in the canneries. It is deplorable that
the women and girls feel the necessity of seeking
employment in these places, for, as a rule, they
work with Chinamen who are the very scum of
their nation, and the native women and girls are
far from being elevated by their contact with
them. Then, too, it is dirty employment and degrading. We would protest if white women and
girls worked in them. The native women and
girls do so because there is practically no other
way for them to get the few dollars they make
in a season. We regret that there is nothing more
elevating in the way of employment for them.

One of the leading industries of the country is
mining. This is a new industry to the native,

having been introduced by the white man. Yet to-day scores of natives are employed in the mines, chiefly at Treadwell and Juneau. Some of them are expert machine-men, capable of handling steam drills with skill, but most of them are mere labourers. They have given good satisfaction as miners, but many of them are averse to working in the mines on account of the danger and the hard work involved. Fishing and hunting, their natural industries, appeal to them more strongly, but hunting and trapping, which once occupied the foremost place in the industries of the Thlingets, have now fallen to third or fourth place. Some never engage in them at all.

The natives living adjacent to the ocean find lucrative employment in hunting the fur-seal and the sea-otter. This 's especially true of the Hydahs, who live near Dixon Entrance, of the Sitkans, who live on Norfolk Sound, and of the Hoonahs, who live on Icy Strait. These all have access to the ocean where the seal and sea-otter are found. When a sea-otter is seen he is quickly surrounded with canoes and speared or shot by native experts. A single otter skin brings from four to eight hundred dollars.

All kinds of land animals are sought by native hunters, but chiefly the deer, bear and fox. The first are killed mainly for food. Their pelts are not now marketable, and when they were they brought only fifty or seventy-five cents apiece. The skin is largely made into moccasins and pouches, adorned with beads, by the native women. Aside from this, little use is made of it.

Bears and foxes are killed mainly for their furs. Bear skins bring from five to forty dollars apiece, according to their quality. The fur of the red fox has little value, but that of the blue, black or silver is very valuable, the silver bringing as high as fourteen and fifteen hundred dollars apiece. Of course these beauties are not caught every day.

Mountain sheep, which a few years ago were plentiful, but are now scarce, are occasionally hunted. The meat of the animal is highly prized, and its fur makes a very desirable rug. They have very little market value. The marten, beaver, mink and land-otter, as well as other fur-bearing animals, are bagged when they cross the native's path. The dressing of animals and the curing of furs are done almost exclusively by the women.

During the great Klondike boom in the year 1898, many took supplies and outfits for prospectors and fortune hunters from the beach up over the famous Chilkoot and White Passes into the Yukon country. Some of them showed wonderful packing ability and made big money at this laborious work.

Carving in wood, silver, horn and stone (black slate) gives employment to some. These carvings are turned out every season for the tourist trade. There is a good demand for them, and not a few dollars are picked up in this way. From the yellow cedar they carve miniature totem poles, canoes, paddles and trinket boxes; from silver coin they make bracelets, rings, spoons, napkin-rings, paper-cutters, butter-knives and stick-pins, all carrying totemic designs; from the horn of the mountain sheep, large spoons with fancy totemic handles; from the slate, totems, pipes and vessels of different designs. A great deal of skill, ingenuity and art is evidenced in these carvings.

A few Thlingets are carpenters and some are cobblers. A few are engaged in business on a small scale. While naturally shrewd traders, very few of them have any talent or inclination for business. They are rarely found in any of the professions. A few of the young women are teachers, having been educated in mission and government schools.

The women, on the whole, are more industrious than the men. In addition to their domestic cares, they manufacture (by hand, of course) mittens, moccasins, baskets and all kinds of beadwork for sale. In the summer time they are very busy putting up food for winter, and in the winter with their sewing and weaving.

The mittens they make are for workmen and retail for twenty-five cents a pair. The back is made of blue or brown denim and the palm of light duck. They are sold at the local stores, as are the moccasins made from the dressed skin of the deer or mountain sheep, the fur of the hairseal, and moose hide, the latter being the most durable. As the moose and mountain sheep are much harder to get than the deer, the deerskin moccasins are most common. They are both plain and fancy, ranging in price from fifty cents a pair to five dollars. The fancy ones are ornamented with beads, and are fleece or fur lined.

Blankets are made of the wool of the mountain sheep and of squirrel skins, the former being known as Chilkat blankets because they originated with the Chilkat natives, and are made chiefly by them. It requires great skill, patience, and months of time to make a single Chilkat blanket. It is a long and tedious process to card the wool and make the yarn and dye it. Then follow months of toil in the weaving.

The pattern is always totemic; on the best blankets it bears the head of the trout (*squatz*). It is painted on a board from three to four feet long and two and a half feet wide. The weaving is done in a frame about five feet long and three feet wide, but the blankets are of different sizes. The weaver sits in front of the frame with her pattern at one side where she can readily see it as she weaves. Her yarns vary in size from a thread to a coarse cord, some being the natural colour while others are black and yellow. These are the only colours, so far as we remember (and we have seen many of them), that ever go into a Chilkat blanket.

The white represents the mountain sheep; the black, the crow, the patron bird of the great Crow fraternity; and the yellow the eagle (whose claws and beak are yellow), the patron bird of the great Eagle fraternity. The Thlinget term for yellow is *tschak*(or *cheth*)-*gin-diya*—eagle-claw colour.

These blankets are worth from seventy-five to one hundred and fifty dollars each, according to the size and workmanship. They will wear indefinitely, so compactly are they woven. The colours used are practically indestructible, as none but native dyes are used in them. They are more ornamental than practical, as they are not used for covering the body as bedding, but originally were made as part of a chief's dancing costume, and to throw over him as he lay in state after death. This was to indicate his rank and high station in life. Only rich and high-caste natives possessed them.

They now have an artistic value as well as or-

MICROCOPY RESOLUTION TEST CHART

(ANSI and ISO TEST CHART No. 2)

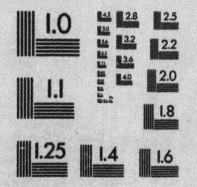

APPLIED IMAGE Inc

1653 East Main Street
Rochester, New York 14609 USA
(716) 482 – 0300 – Phone
(716) 288 – 5989 – Fax

namental, showing what natural artists some of these natives are. The patterns are faultlessly woven into the blanket, entirely by eye, a feat requiring nice skill. We have watched the weaver by the hour as she deftly wove her yarns into this artistic fabric, and wondered how she could follow the design so accurately just by glancing at the pattern on the board. Wealthy tourists purchase these Chilkat blankets as fine specimens of native art and workmanship, using them to ornament their curio corners.

Squirrel robes were once plentiful, but now it does not pay to make them. From seventy to a hundred skins of the chattering little fellows are sewed together in such a manner as to make the robe look like one large fur. At one time these robes could be bought for two dollars apiece, the amount hardly covering the cost of the ammunition used in killing the squirrels. As they are rarely seen now, they have advanced largely in price.

Various kinds of beadwork are made for the market, and these help to swell the financial receipts of the women. Moccasins, pouches and various articles used in the dance are ornamented with beads. In early times all designs were totemic, but now they are taken from fashion-plates, catalogues, wall-paper and other places. While some of this work is really artistic, most of it is poor and commands little money. The tourists buy little of it, as their great hobby is baskets.

Some years ago the women were skilled in making *suck-a-chew* (pottery). Scarcely a trace of this art can now be found. Like rope-making, it has fallen into desuetude.

Yäk(canoe)-building, which at one time was a

thriving industry, is now practically a back number. There were regular builders who constructed them and put them on the market to meet the demand, which was heavy.

Canoes are frail and not durable. Their greatest enemy is the sun, and the natives must either cover them over or keep them wet when exposed to it. If travelling when the sun shines, they frequently fill their bailing-shell with water and throw it all over the canoe. When ashore, they keep the canoes covered with blankets, boards, brush or grass to protect them. If they lived in a land of much sunshine it would be almost impossible to keep their canoes a month. As it is, though they live in a land of clouds and rain, they have a hard time to protect them.

Canoe-building demanded much skill from the workman, and his product commanded big money. Some canoes brought four or five hundred dollars apiece. No matter how large, every one was built out of a solid log—generally of yellow cedar. The adz was the principal tool used. Indeed, few and rude were the tools employed in early times, and yet fine workmanship was done.

The log is first dug out until it roughly resembles a canoe. It is then filled with water and this is heated with hot stones. The wood thus steamed becomes pliable, and braces are put in to hold it to the desired shape. This accomplished, the workman finishes the job by chipping and chipping and sandpapering (literally dog-fish-papering, as dogfish skin was used before real sandpaper was introduced to the natives), until the craft with its beautiful lines is ready for the sea.

The braces are left in and are used in lieu of seats, but in the days of the paddle, the usual seat was the bottom of the craft. This accounts for many of the natives having misshapen legs. Until long after the white man came, canoes were propelled entirely with paddles. Gradually oars were introduced, and now they are propelled by the combination of oars and paddle, except when the sail is brought into service. Every native uses his sail whenever he can, as rowing or paddling is no pastime with him.

The women are as expert in handling the canoe as the men. They invariably act as captain, sitting in the stern of the craft. Though the little ship may have a rudder, yet the captain always has a paddle in her hand to use when required. Often the women travel by themselves, especially in the berry season. Men disdain picking berries, considering that the work of women. But the women are the most independent of people and so go off alone for berries and also for cockles, clams, mussels and other sea food.

It is a marvel how big, heavy, clumsy women manage getting in and out of the small canoes without capsizing them. But they do.

We are acquainted with a woman who one night, all alone, sailed a canoe a distance of seventy miles with two dead people in it. They had been poisoned by eating mussels, and she took the long, lonely journey in order to reach their people.

The women being experts with the paddle and handy with the oars, they are genuine helpmeets to their husbands when travelling.

Canoes are of all sizes. Some will not carry more than two persons, while others will carry forty or fifty. When nicely ballasted, these will weather rough seas and heavy winds.

The prows of some are proudly decorated with

totemic designs, war-canoes being generally thus
treated. A chief named Samhat, living at Kassan,
gave to the District of Alaska a large war-canoe
of this type. It is forty-seven feet long, more
than six feet across the beam, and three and one-
half feet deep. It is now kept with other relics
at Sitka.

During the days of native warfare, these proud
monarchs of the deep were looked upon as possessing intelligence and sharing the honour of
victories and the shame of defeat. Sometimes
they were smashed by the defeated tribe, as if in
some way to blame.

For beauty of line, the high-class native canoes
are hard to beat. The model was suggested to
the natives by the breast bone of the mallard
duck. The wishbone of the duck suggested the
snowshoe, which at one time was largely made and
used by these people.

For years, on national holidays when sports
were indulged in, the canoe-race was the most
attractive feature of the day. Each canoe had
a crew of twelve or fourteen men, and from three
to five canoes generally entered the race. The
distance covered was from three to four miles.
Every native in the race was in shirt sleeves with
bare head. As soon as the signal to start was
given, the paddles of each boat dipped simultane-
ously into the water and this uniformity of stroke
was maintained throughout the entire course. At
every stroke the canoe was almost literally lifted
out of the water. As they crossed the line at the
finish, every paddle was lifted upright and a loud
huzza went up from the throats of the contestants.
This was especially true of the victorious crew,
who would proudly pocket their prize of a hundred

to a hundred and fifty dollars. These races will
stand out in the memory of all who ever saw them,
as they were sports of unusual attraction.

As totem poles are practically no longer erected,
this industry is at an end.

The Thlingets never had, and probably never
will have, any extensive commercial activities.
The trading they did among themselves was in-
considerable. The common method of obtaining
property was by force (war), condemnation proceedings on the grounds of injury, or insults, and
entail through death. The little trading that was
carried on between the Thlingets and the Sticks,
or Interior, Indians was controlled by the haughty
Chilkats. Even this traffic ceased years ago, the
Klondike gold discovery being responsible for it.

The Interior Indians were rich in furs which
were coveted by the Thlingets. The latter would
carry prints, blankets and other articles not too
difficult to pack, over the coast mountain range
and into the country of the Sticks and barter them
for furs. These they would get on their own
terms, as the Sticks were a spiritless class and
easily intimidated by the Thlingets. This traffic
never amounted to much.

A Takou chief, whose home was at Juneau, and
who was drowned some years ago, once did a
thriving business with a trading schooner. He
would send to Portland, Oregon, for two or three
thousand dollars worth of goods at a time. He
would take his stock to various villages and dispose of it at a handsome profit. He was shrewd,
calculating and unscrupulous enough to take every
advantage possible. He accumulated several
thousand dollars before his death, but no other
native has conducted a similar enterprise.

BASKETS

There are no capitalists among these natives.
Seemingly they do not know how to handle large
sums of money. If they get any amount of it they
hoard it rather than invest it. The promise of
interest and income from investments has little
or no weight with them. Only immediate results
appeal to the average native mind. They are extremely suspicious of one another, and for this
reason will not combine and form companies for
their mutual advantage.

Until quite recently nothing along this line has
been attempted. Some months ago the United
States Government encouraged the natives of
Hydaburg (a settlement of Hydah-speaking aborigines) to form a stock company to operate a
store in that village. Some of the Thlingets, hearing of this enterprise, have recently imitated their
Hydah brethren by combining to operate stores,
one such company having been formed at Klawock and one at Klukwan. As these are in their
experimental stage, it remains to be seen what
success they meet. Since they will have little, if
any, patronage aside from the members themselves, it is clear that they will not get very much
out of them but what they themselves put in, and
will never amass any great amount of wealth from
such combinations. It may, however, be good
training for them, and while they will not make
much, they will not lose much.

But the white man is everywhere operating. He
has in every way the advantage of his Thlinget
brother; to meet him in business competition will
be no easy task. In fact the chance for a native
to accumulate much wealth in enterprises confined
to his own people is very small. He has a better
chance if he puts his money into enterprises car-

ried on by white men. But until his confidence in
the white man is stronger than it is at present
he will not do this.

We have substantial banks in Alaska where natives might deposit some of their earnings and accumulate a little capital with which to engage in
money-making enterprises, but they will not avail
themselves of the opportunity. This is due largely
to a want of confidence. They can never hope to
attain to opulence and plenty until, like the white
man, they make money as well as their hands work
for them. Up to the present they have depended
entirely on their hands for means, hence as to
wealth they are not very rich per capita. There
are money-making enterprises in their midst.
Their investments in these would be welcomed.
And while they would stand a chance of losing,
they would also stand a chance of gaining. But,
lacking confidence, they venture nothing.

IX

BASKETRY

OF all the industries common to women the
making of baskets is by far the most extensive. One can scarcely enter a house
without seeing women engaged in weaving them.
Prices have advanced within the last decade several hundred per cent. Baskets that could have
been bought ten years ago for five dollars would
now bring twenty dollars. This has given an im-
petus to those who make them, but this, like other
native arts, is on the wane.

If they were paid in proportion to the time it
takes to make the baskets, prices would have to
advance still higher. It takes time and labour to
procure the raw material, which consists of the
tender roots of the young spruce tree and certain
grasses; to soften the former by soaking and
steaming to make them pliable and workable; to
prepare the dyes and dye the straws the different
colours; to split and trim the roots and grasses
into fine and coarse strands, and then to weave
them into the finished article.

This being so, we can little wonder that the
rising generation of girls, who are learning the
white man's value of time and who have other
opportunities of earning money, take little or no
interest in basket-weaving. It is an industry
mostly engaged in by elderly Thlinget women, and

when these have passed away basket-making will
be practically at an end.

The summer tourist trade in baskets is very
large, and wealthy tourists are responsible for the
prevailing high prices.

There are baskets, and baskets—that is, there
are some coarse and worthless and some fine and
valuable. Every community has its fine and
coarse weavers, its amateurs and its real artists
in weaving.

Lieutenant G. T. Emmons has published an interesting work on native basketry which every
connoisseur should read. We think that he claims
too much, in asserting that every design on a
basket has special significance. It is true that
many have. It is no less true that some have been
copied from patterns seen on blankets, on wall-
paper and on other objects. In earlier days all
designs were native and totemic, but this is not
true of all seen to-day.

Baskets are named and known to all natives
according to the chief design they bear, their
weave, the material they are made of, their
shape, the size, or the use to which they are
put.

The basket with this design, ⧓, is called
kŏn-nāst', meaning the cross; with this, ▼▼▼
kluk-shā-yă-kee'gē, meaning half berry; with this,
◆ thlă-kā-dă-di'shē, which is the name of the
bat, who is diamond-shape when his wings are
stretched out; with this, ➤ ä-hän'ē, meaning
arrow-head; with this, ⧓ klee (blanket)-wän-
kŭs-ă-ä'yă, meaning blanket pattern; with this,
ⲧⲟⲟ tsŏw(hat)-sŏk-toot'zē, meaning dancing
hat pattern; with either of these designs, ⧓
ⲧⲟⲟ, it is called shă-di-yă-ä'gē, meaning dancing

basket, as either design is worn on dancing hats
made of the basket material.

When named according to the weave, *chäk-chĕ-
wŏn-kă-see'dĕ* (tendon in the eagle's claw) is the
name of the basket with a cord-like raise running
around it. It is so called because in early times
this cord was taken from the claw of the eagle.
Wăk-ŭs-kŏt' is the name of the open or lattice-
work basket; *woosh-tă-kä'gĕ* of the closely woven,
water-tight basket; *kŏk-să-hä'dy* of the basket
made with plain stitches close together; *woosh-
tă-hä'gy* of the one with plain stitches underneath
the figure; *kŏt-ät-thlē'ky* of the one with the rim
finished in a certain way, and *kŏk-ĕ-sŭt'* of the one
with the bottom finished in a certain style.

The names, according to shape, are: *too-dă-
hook'*, the covered basket; so called because of the
stones taken from the craw of the grouse and put
in the top of the lid. When the lid is shaken the
stones rattle. Stones gathered anywhere else
cannot be used for this purpose. *.'ölth* is the
name of a large shallow basket used for catching
berries when they are shaken from the bush,
which is the usual mode of gathering huckleberries. *Woostă-dă-kŭt-tzoo'* is the name of the
basket that is made entirely of straw. The word
means "all straw."

The Thlingets originally had no weights and
measures. Everything sold, or exchanged, was
by the chunk, or piece, or basket. Hence to distinguish the sizes of baskets the largest was called
chew-kăt', the next size *yä'nah*, and the size used
for stringing around the neck and picking berries
in and which when filled was dumped into a large
one, was called *să-kă-tŏn'ny.*

Woosh-to-quä'gĕ is the name given to the

merely plain basket without any design, and kä-
gĕ-sŭt' (three roots) is another name given to a
slightly different basket.

From the above, the reader is not to infer that
only three sizes of baskets are made. Far from
it. The sizes are legion—from the capacity of
a thimble to a bushel or more. The sizes
mentioned were more as gauges of measure-
ment.

Then baskets are named according to what they
are used for. Kŏt means strainer and is the name
of the openwork basket used for straining oils.
Naukth is the name of a basket made from the
bark of a tree and used as a gunny sack for holding potatoes.

Baskets are now made of all sizes, shapes and
styles. Some represent tea-kettles or stew-pots;
some are oblong or round, and flaring from the
bottom up; some are deep and some are shallow.
Bottles and canes are beautifully covered with
basket material, and small mats and hats, used
principally in dancing, are made of it. Some of
these are very expensive, costing as high as forty
dollars apiece.

Baskets used for cooking prior to the advent
of the iron pot, were plain, without any design,
and strongly made.

There is a mammoth basket kept at Kluckwan
that is called the Mother-of-baskets. The natives
have a tradition that this is the progenitor of all
baskets. Several women worked on it at the same
time. No one is allowed to make so large a one
now.

The baskets bearing the native dyes are far
more valuable, other work being equal, than those
that have the common diamond dyes, as the na-

NATIVES VENDING CURIOS

tive dyes are much more durable. They remain bright indefinitely.

The brilliant yellow seen in baskets and in the famous Chilkat blankets is obtained from a moss that grows on certain trees. Green is obtained from copper rocks and from a common weed. Its leaves are boiled and the liquid makes a bright green dye. They get the red from certain red berries, and purple from blueberries.

The most durable and brilliant black is that of natural black straws found in the bottom of certain lakes. There is a black made from soot and other ingredients, but it is inferior to the natural black straw. Brown is obtained from strong urine.

Baskets coloured with any of these native dyes are not so common as are those with the ordinary dyes, and many buy baskets without a question as to whether the dyes are native or not.

One of the most particular pieces of work in connection with fine basket-weaving is splitting the fibre and straws. This requires much practice and skill in order to make them uniform. And if the straws are not uniform in size the work is uneven and botchy. Certain old women are very dexterous in making fine fibres and straws. They have a clam-shaped piece of steel, the edge of which is very sharp. With this they split the fibre, take the end of one in the mouth while they cleverly work the other off with their fingers. The trick is to make the strands as nearly uniform as possible without wasting the material. If it breaks off too short, or runs thick and then thin, it is rejected.

Basket-weavers sit with the legs outright on the floor with the basket in the lap, and in a stooping posture with one knee down and the other up. Some women are very round-shouldered because of this habit. All designs are woven in the basket without any pattern before them. It is all taken from the mind and is a marvel of accuracy on this account. Very intricate designs are often made, and yet with such precision as if the basket had been stamped with a die. This is the real marvel in basket-weaving. The fineness consists in getting fine fibre and close weaving, but working in the patterns or designs is a matter of nice mental calculation, accuracy of vision and discrimination of just proportions.

The bottom of the basket is first made. When this is completed a piece of cardboard, the same size as the bottom, is sewed on the inner side. This is done to stiffen it, that the upper part may be worked to better advantage. Beside the weaver is a vessel of water into which she thrusts her fingers every minute or so while she is weaving, to keep the fibre moist and pliable. If too dry, it does not work well.

Every woman is the vendor of her own baskets. On the arrival of steamers they take their stock in hand and make for the wharves. Some advantageous point is selected so as to catch the eye of the traveller. There they sit without a word until spoken to. If they know nothing of the English they are handicapped, unless an English-speaking native is near. But a little knowledge of it enables them to carry on their trade. They have a uniform price for their wares, seldom making any reduction. They seem unconcerned whether they sell their products or not. You may take them or leave them. All is quiet, and no effort is put forth to induce the prospective purchaser to buy. If he buys, and puts down the price, well and good. If he does not it is all the same.

No matter at what hour the steamer arrives, be it two o'clock in the morning, the native curio vendor is there to do business.

It is an interesting sight to see anywhere from six to a dozen native girls and women squatting along the passage-way as one leaves or boards the steamer with their wares such as baskets, bead-work, carvings, etc., spread out to view on the sidewalk or ground.

And, as this trade is entirely with the tourists, it behooves them to meet all tourist-carrying steamers no matter what hour their arrival. It is a traffic which brings them in a good revenue, and the old women especially are right on to the job. In sunshine or rain, day or night, when the steamer lands they are lined up ready for business.

X

TRAITS

ONE of the most conspicuous traits of the Thlinget is independence. What he wants to do he will do, as a rule. He lives for the present, and gratifies the desires of the hour, no matter what it may cost him. If given his choice whether to accept five dollars at once or fifty dollars a year hence, although reasonably certain that he could have the fifty dollars, he would accept the five, and be done with it. The NOW appeals to him. No job, however lucrative, holds him if he wants a holiday, or a lay-off to hunt, or even to loaf. Because of this trait, he is unreliable as an employé. Without a moment's notice, he will throw up his job and leave; and it may be at a time when his services are most needed. But he cares neither about the inconvenience he may make his employer nor the loss that falls upon himself. A white man thinks twice before he throws up his job. Not so with the Thlinget. His desires, more than his needs, control him.

Nothing galls him like being " bossed " or controlled. To him it is a species of slavery, and the slave is the lowest of all beings, in his estimation. It is for this reason that the people make poor and unreliable servants. The native girl who is hired as a domestic servant does not stay long. She wants her own way, to go off and return when

she pleases, and chafes under commands or restrictions.

This independent nature of the native should
not surprise us when we remember that he has
grown up, practically speaking, in absolute free-
dom, even in childhood.

Vanity is another Thlinget trait. They are very
fond of military uniforms, caps and badges. Not
a few join the Salvation Army that they may
wear its caps and uniforms. We know a certain
chief who changed his clothes several times while
the transient tourist steamer was lying at the
wharf, in order to display his suits. He would
appear at the steamer and parade around until
he was satisfied that he had been observed in all
of his finery. He had military suits bedecked
with badges, priestly suits (Russian), and other
remarkable garments, all mainly for show. No
peacock ever strutted around with more vanity
than he.

For vainglory they often destroy their own
property. We have seen fine canoes demolished
with an axe in a few moments of time; dishes,
stoves and other household goods smashed by
their proud owner, just that he might be considered a greater man than some other. In the days
of slavery, owners of slaves vied with one another
in the sacrifice of slaves. Slaves were property,
and the owner who destroyed the most was considered the greatest man. Potlatches are given more
for vainglory than for anything else. Public
praise and honour are the objects in view.

Because oolikan oil is a luxury, and costly,
chiefs spatter their canoe sails with it to indicate
that they are rich enough to waste the article.

Touchiness, or sensitiveness, is another conspicuous trait of the Thlinget. He often takes offence when none is intended. He is very sensitive to slights, innuendoes, rebukes, blame, censure, shame and ridicule.

He takes offence if he is asked to do the slightest service for one whom he regards as of a lower caste than himself, or to perform any service without compensation, if his proffered gift is refused, or if one objects to any of his food.

If, out of sympathy, you say to a widow, "It is too bad you lost your husband," she takes offence. She regards it as an insinuation that she poisoned him, or did something to kill him.

But the most cutting thing of all to a Thlinget is to be laughed at or ridiculed. He fairly burns with shame at this. He has a sick *tumtum* (heart) for days and days, and if the offender is a native he is sometimes compelled to pay for the offence.

White people who are not familiar with the ways of the natives may very innocently offend them. Indeed their warmest white friends have not infrequently done this.

They are very sensitive to insults, and demand apologies, with payment for their wounded feelings. Generally a feast is given and the offence atoned for by a proper money payment. One man saw another encroaching on what he considered his fishing ground. He went to the trespasser, seized his gaff and broke it in pieces. This was a grave insult to the man who owned the gaff-hook, but he did not then resent it. His tribe, however, took it up, and in due time proper apologies were made, with a large payment to the offended party.

A certain chief was highly indignant because

others had received invitations to attend a certain feast before himself. He went around the community storming about it. The feast was held some thirty miles away, and he absolutely refused to attend because of this breach of etiquette. His, too, would have been the lion's share in the distribution of goods at the feast.

The Thlingets regard it as a shameful thing to have the face cut or scratched by another. Such an injury must be atoned for by a big money consideration, and it is a disgrace to the injured one and his tribe if they do not persist until the injury has been paid for. Consequently all natives receiving such injuries never let up on the perpetrator and his tribe until a satisfactory settlement has been effected. Hounding is one of their characteristics. A creditor pursues his debtor until the uttermost farthing is paid, nor does the injured forgive or forget, nor cease to clamour until he has had his redress. Not to be paid for an injury is a great shame.

It is a matter of shame to a Thlinget to have his opponent in a quarrel destroy at the time more personal property than he does. This shows who is the richer man or woman, or the one who has the greater contempt for property. The defeated one has the contempt of all the community.

Two women were quarrelling. In a rage one of them said to the other, " I'll shut you up! " At that she rushed into her house, came out with both hands full of silver money and scattered it to the crowd that was watching the proceedings. This did shut the mouth of her opponent, as she could not do likewise.

A man in an altercation shoved a chief's wife and she fell. The chief owned a number of slaves.

As soon as the wronged woman informed her husband, he sought revenge by heaping a greater shame upon the man who gave the insult, accomplishing it by making a public sacrifice of some of his slaves. As the man who offered the insult had no slaves to sacrifice, he was thus put to everlasting shame. So now when natives quarrel it is a common thing for one to say to the other, "Shut up! You might be like Mitkeen," that is, have nothing to destroy in order to get even.

To be called a slave, or a witch, is a shame to any native, and sometimes leads to bloodshed. It is a great shame to any native if one speaks contemptuously of his grandmother. There is no insult which he will more quickly resent than this.

The Thlingets are revengeful. An injury is never forgotten or forgiven with most of them until in some way they have had revenge. An eye for an eye, and a tooth for a tooth, has been, and still is, an established principle with them. It may be long before they strike back, but they surely will some day. The Sitkans waited years to avenge the massacre of their men by the Wrangell natives. But the day of revenge came, and the slaughter was fearful.

Jealousy is another of their traits. On mere suspicion wives have been cruelly beaten and disfigured for life by their husbands. Women are sometimes fearfully jealous of each other. When so, each tries to disfigure the other.

The Thlingets are very crafty. They resort to all sorts of schemes by which to get money or property for themselves. Matters that were supposed settled years ago are raked up and made the basis for a money claim. They will force some insignificant and undesirable present on another,

and in due time demand five or ten times as much
in return. Some article is given for the dead,
and after the funeral the relatives of the deceased
give ten times as much in return. The most absurd claims are made for money. A native who
owned an interest in a well-paying old mine was
hounded for money by a woman, on the ground
that she and her people used to fish in the stream
near the gold mine. Another woman insisted on
a man paying her some money because at one time
she prayed (so she claimed) for the superintendent of the Training School to take his sister into
the school. ʻ urged that it was owing to her
prayer that the sister was taken in, and the girl's
education was, therefore, due to her. For this
reason she claimed that the brother should pay
her some money.

Some put on a pool face when they have scores
of blankets stored away and much money hoarded
up. They seem to think that the missionary is
their legitimate prey, that he came among them
to open his purse to them whenever he is appealed
to. If he refuses, as he is often obliged to do,
he is "Kla-oosh-ka" (no good).

The Thlinget is usually very politic, temporiz-
ing according as he believes it is his personal interest or not. The public weal never appeals to
him. Cunning and deceit are thought smart and
considered commendable. In trade, the white
man has to be shrewd to outwit the average
Thlinget.

Seldom do we find an avaricious native. On the
contrary, he is inclined to extravagance and to be
a spendthrift. If he saves, it is not for the love
of hoarding, but that he may give the more, in
due time, at a feast. As a rule, he spends freely

and saves little, believing in the Epicurean doctrine—the present gratification of fleshly desires.

Fickleness is a trait of the native mind. In this respect the natives are very muc'. like children. They make a bargain and close the deal. Afterwards they repent of the bargain, demand to trade back and generally manage to do so. The native may be your friend to-day and your worst enemy to-morrow. He changes his mind for very slight reasons. He lacks, as a rule, any sense of honour in holding to his promises, contracts or bargains. You may befriend him all you please, but if you offend him, or cross him, in anything, he will forget all you have done for him and reward you with ill will.

"One fairly wearies," writes a government teacher, in one of her official reports, "of an effort to protect them. They can lie so successfully and they will go against the missionary and the government teacher and all who are trying to help and uplift them, and will stand by the one who furnishes them the intoxicants—and why? Because they want to seek it yet again."

They are inclined to be stolid and undemonstrative in the presence of white strangers, but among themselves they are loquacious, lively and full of fun and laughter. They have wonderful control of their feeling. If taken to New York City, though filled with wonder at the sights, they would maintain as much indifference as if they had always lived there. We have taken Thlinget children to the States and when we arrived at Seattle, have looked for some expressions of surprise and wonder on their faces. But no change was visible, nor could we discover the slightest emotion.

Endurance of bodily pain, especially by the women, is a characteristic trait. In order to bear pain without a groan, they often put a stick between their teeth to bite on. Even children are taught to bear bodily pain bravely. The writer saw an old woman walk barefoot to the beach and wade into the water up to her knees with floating ice all around her, get into a canoe, take her seat with bare, cold feet and paddle off, and at the very moment the thermometer was only seven degrees above zero.

When loved ones die, grief takes strong hold upon them, but it is ephemeral. So poignant at times is their grief that they throw themselves into the fire, tear out their hair, stupefy themselves with liquor and even commit suicide.

Kindred have strong affection for one another. This is especially true of parents and children. If any member of the family is seriously ill, no matter how far away the others may be, they will go to him if they have the means to do so. Parents are very considerate of their children when they are sick. Sick natives in our hospitals at Juneau are often visited by their relatives who live many miles away. They are tender in their ministrations to the dying, and show deep sympathy for one who meets with any serious bodily injury.

Hospitality, another conspicuous trait of these people, will be considered in the chapter on totemism.

Sociability is one of their strong points. One of the severest punishments to a native is to compel him to live apart from his people. Men who have been sent to penitentiaries in the States have soon died after their incarceration. No

Thlinget will live in solitude by himself, like a white man.

Many of them have sunny dispositions and are full of humour and wit. Among themselves they are continually joking, laughing and making funny remarks. We have been with them in camp and in their homes, have frequently been at their socials, and can truly say that never have *we* seen a people, as a class, take life so happily, evince more humour and bubble over more with laughter.

They are excessively fond of all kinds of amusements. In their socials they play all kinds of games that provoke laughter. They are very imitative, and are born mimics and mockers. Native children in our missions show great skill in " taking off " the fastidious and inquisitive tourists, and in assuming certain attitudes and tones of the white people.

These people are very observant, though you could scarcely detect them when they are making some of their most critical observations. A glance at a person and they know what he has on from head to foot. His complexion, facial features, any peculiarities about him, rings, chains, in short, everything about him is taken in. A native girl was assaulted by a white man. The struggle to escape him, which was successful, was only for a moment, yet in that moment of time, and though she was labouring under excitement, she noted him so well that there was no trouble in identifying him. She even described a ring he wore. It was the first time she had ever seen the man.

They are also extremely clever in reading human nature and very fluent in speech. They are never at a loss to express themselves. In prayer-meetings, where they invariably take part in speaking and praying, they show a power of expression that many public white speakers might well envy. Among them are several very able orators in their own tongue. It is proverbial that a woman has a lively tongue, and this surely holds good with the Thlinget women. When quarrelling, as they do all too frequently, their flow of language is very surprising—and none too delicate.

They employ much imagery, and their rhetoric is often very flowery. Before coming to the point they beat about the bush, commencing their remarks with some ancient history of their ancestors.

In their homes and among themselves they have a habit of all talking at the same time; and yet they seem to be able not to confuse one another and able to distinguish what each has said. We have heard six or more, all labouring under excitement and jabbering away, and yet each had a clear knowledge of what all the others said.

They are not bloodthirsty, nor is treachery a pronounced trait. It is true that they have secretly killed white people, but not from treachery, but from their inexorable law of life for life. And it matters not whose life it is, so it be one of the race of the one who took a life from them.

While gratitude is not a marked trait of this people, yet many of them are possessed with this grace. We have evidences of this in the possession of some of their handiwork which gratitude prompted them to give us. Baskets, silver spoons, rings, beadwork, small totem poles, curios of one kind and another, and even a solid gold watch worth forty-five dollars have been given the author as a token of their esteem and an expression of their gratitude. Their personal photographs, numbering more than a hundred, have also been given him for the same reason.

I think oftentimes they appreciate favours done them, but lack the grace of expressing their appreciation. It is only just, however, to say that the better educated evince, and that in a very graceful manner, their appreciation of all favours done them. It must be acknowledged that there are those, and not a few, who show no gratitude whatever and seem to think any favour shown them is their due. But to assert, as some do, that they are absolutely devoid and incapable of gratitude, is incorrect, to say the least. The Thlinget, as has been shown, is not a very demonstrative personage, and this accounts to some extent for his seeming lack of gratitude.

XI

FOOD

ALTHOUGH the Thlingets live in a country that has an inhospitable climate, yet the Creator has endowed it with a great variety of foodstuffs. Its waters teem with fish the year through, its woods with game, and its soil is productive of vegetables and small fruits.

Fish constitute the principal food of the natives, as it is the most abundant and most easily procured of all foods in Alaska.

While there is a variety of fish to draw from, yet salmon is by far the most popular and the most abundantly used.

There are five varieties of this species, the king, silver, sock-eye, humpback and dog-salmon. The humpback is more largely cured by the natives for winter use than any other. As fresh fish, the red salmon is most largely used.

The red and silver salmon are caught with hook and line or with net, while the humpback and dog-salmon are caught with gaff-hook or net. The humpback and dog-salmon are caught mostly in shallow streams. When caught, they are turned over to the women, who clean and cut them into slices, after removing the bones, and then hang them on wooden frames to be dried by the wind and sun. After they are thoroughly cured they are tied up in bundles and stored away for winter use.

The halibut are treated in the same way as the salmon, but not so largely used for curing purposes, as they can get them fresh the year round.

The natives consider the humpback the most palatable of the salmon species.

Herring, *oolikan* (candle-fish), and seal are also staple fish foods. They make but very little use of the other varieties of fish, such as cod, tom-cod, flounder, trout, bass, etc.

The herring are caught with a rake the teeth of which are perpendicular rather than horizontal. It is a pole eight or ten feet long, the lower end being blade-shaped so it may cut easily through the water. The teeth project from the sharper edge of this blade in a row two or three feet long. While a canoe is being paddled along by one native another uses this rake. He thrusts it down into the school of herring, gives it a sweep through the school, impaling as many as he can on the sharp teeth, and then draws it up and dumps his catch into the canoe. In a short time he can fill a small canoe in this manner. The herring are prized not so much for the meat as for their oil. This is boiled out of them and put into cans and boxes for winter use.

Fish and seal oils are important staples of food. Some bear oil is used, but not to any great extent. The principal oils of the Thlingets are extracted from the herring and *oolikan*, the latter furnishing the most desirable.

While the herring are taken almost the year round, the *oolikan* appear in the spring only, and then for but two or three weeks. They come into certain rivers in great schools, literally cramming them. They are scooped out of the river with a dip-net, and dumped into a large hole in the ground to " mellow " (rot). It is claimed that the oil comes out of them better when in a state of putrefaction. This is not considered a detraction in any way, but rather adds excellence to the taste, just as some highly civilized people prefer cheese flavoured with skippers and fowl mellowed with age.

When sufficiently " ripe," the *oolikan* are taken out of the hole and put into a small canoe which is used as a caldron. Hot stones are thrown among the fish to try the oil out, and this is put into boxes or cans of about five gallons capacity and stored away for winter use. When cool it has about the same colour and consistency as butter, and is practically the butter of the people. They scarcely eat a meal without using oil. The Thlinget dips his bread, biscuit and dried fish into it and puts up his berries for winter use in it. His body is so saturated with it through use as to make his skin shiny and almost impervious to the cold. Seldom do natives freeze to death, though often exposed to cold that no white man could endure without an abundance of warm clothes to protect him.

The herring are treated in a different way from the *oolikan*. While fresh they are put into large iron pots (in earlier times into large baskets) and hot stones are thrown in with them to boil the grease out. It is put up in the same way as that from the *oolikan*, and is of about the same colour and consistency as molasses, only not so sluggish in movement.

The herring spawn, while it lasts—which is for a month or more in the spring—is eagerly sought and feasted on in its raw state, just as it is taken from the sea. Herring have particular spawning grounds to which they resort every spring. They will not spawn elsewhere. Every object in the water—shells, rocks, seaweed, pebbles, the ground at the place of spawning—is covered with their minute eggs, the spawn coating every object from a quarter of an inch to half an inch thick. The natives throw branches of the hemlock tree into the water for the spawn to catch on, and these are brought out of the water literally weighted down with the delicacy. The spawn is then exposed to the sun until cured, a process which colours it like gold. The spawning grounds are an interesting sight when the natives are curing these infinitesimal eggs for future use. The small trees look as if they had taken on their autumnal colours when it is nothing more than the sun-dried herring spawn hanging on them.

After it is so cured, they soak it in water. This loosens it from the twigs, and then they throw it into their mouths with their fingers.

The salmon roe is also put up in oil for winter use. This, like the *oolikan*, is allowed to mellow before it is mixed with oil for the winter feasting. The mellowing feature is a very popular one with the natives. Salmon heads are buried in the ground and left there for days until they become good and ripe. They are then taken out and, without any further cooking, devoured with the zest with which a hungry urchin would devour a piece of pumpkin pie. The odour from this delectable dish is so pungent that the ordinary white man could not possibly stand around while the meal is going on. The odour from the herring while in process of cooking, though by no means weak, is tame indeed as compared with that

which emanates from the juicy, ground-baked fish
heads. But when it comes to pungent odours,
that of the *oolikan* scraps beats them all. So
penetrating and durable is it that the holes in
which they were mellowed years ago still send
forth a smell which, when it strikes the nostrils,
makes a man involuntarily reach up and compress
his nose. No slaughter-house nor glue factory
can turn out an odour equal to the *oolikan* ground.
Most Americans who have ever had a whiff of it
will walk miles out of their way, if need be, to
avoid the grounds where this odoriferous little
oolikan is treated for its oil.

Certain portions of the snout of the humpback
salmon, and the head and tail of the silver fish,
are frequently eaten raw. But it is not done because the natives are particularly fond of those
parts. They do it because it is said that the crow,
a long time ago, cooked these parts, and so they
are edible just as they come out of the water.

If you ask a native how he can endure raw fish,
he will ask the white man how he can eat raw
oysters or " live " cheese. Neither of these delicacies of the white man could reach the palate of
a native.

Hair-seal (*tsa*) and fur-seal (*goon*) are not only
used as food, but are prized for their oil. What
pork is to the white man, seal meat is to the native.
In land animals, the principal meat used is
venison. The deer abound in the Thlinget's country, and are easily killed. Venison, as well as
fish, is sun-dried and put up for future use, but
not in such quantities as is fish. Porcupines,
ground-hogs and bears are very plentiful and their
meat is largely used. The meat of the mountain
sheep is highly prized, but they are far more dif-

ficult to kill than any other animal, as they browse on top of almost inaccessible cliffs, practically defying the hunter. Sections of country that once abounded with them now never see them.

The lakes and marshes of southeastern Alaska fairly teem, at times, with wild fowl, such as geese, mallard and other ducks. The natives make but very little use of such, as they do not care to bother with picking and dressing them.

Clams, cockles, mussels and crabs are plentiful, and the natives are fond of them all, especially of a big rock barnacle known as "gum-boot." They will boil out a bushel or more of cockles or clams at a time. Then they string them on sticks, or string, to be eaten as desired. They will keep a number of days, even in the summer, thus prepared. When we have been out with the people on their jaunts, we have shared with them cockles and clams so prepared. Any one who is fond of boiled clams will like them.

Crabs and mussels are both boiled and roasted, and are relished either way by the natives. Both crabs and clams attain wonderful size. We have seen crabs that measured fifty-four inches from the tip of one leg to the tip of the other and weighed fifteen pounds each; and clams (called "yes" in the native tongue) six or seven inches in diameter.

The small-sized scuttle, or devil, fish is very highly prized as a food. The tentacles are fried or boiled. It is claimed by the natives that this is a very delicate morsel.

Berries, of which there are no fewer than thirty varieties, form an important part of the food supplies. They grow wild and some of them in great abundance. Tons upon tons of the finest huckleberries, high-bush cranberries, nagoon berries, salmonberries, and other kinds go to waste every season. There are four or five varieties of huckleberries, two of salmonberries, two of cranberries and three of currants. Then there are strawberries, raspberries, thimbleberries, soap-berries and others.

Huckleberries, nagoon berries and cranberries are put up in fish oil in great quantities for winter use.

The soap-berry is also put up, but not in oil, and when used it is put into a washbowl, a dishpan or a large wooden chopping-bowl, and beaten vigorously with the open hand into a cream which resembles in appearance, when ready to eat, strawberry ice cream, only it is light as foam. Both men and women whip these berries with their hands, their sleeves rolled up to the elbows, the hand being buried in the succulent mess as it is swished around beating it into a cream. When one tires at the job another takes a turn at it. Thus they keep it up until it is ready to eat. Half a dozen sit around a bowl of soap-berries, each helping himself with a spoon as often as he likes.

Crabapples were once largely eaten, but since the introduction of the white man's fruits (apples, oranges, peaches, etc.) they make no use of them.

Very few of the imported fruits used by the white people are eaten by the natives. The apple is the most popular. Certain canned fruits, the peach, pear and apricots, are also used. Pickles, mustard and condiments of all kinds find no place in the Thlinget's diet. Even salt is rejected.

The principal vegetables used are potatoes and turnips. These they raise themselves as well as buy them. Cabbage is eaten both raw and cooked.

They cook a wild rice which is bulbous in its nature and taken from the ground. A popular native vegetable which grows wild is *yä-nǎ̃'äte* (celery). This matures in May, and is gathered by the armload and eaten as we eat celery, only without salt. We have seen women and children with their laps full of it, eating away until the whole was consumed. They peal the outer skin off and eat the inner stem of the plant, which resembles the pumpkin stalk.

Another article of diet is the white, or inner, bark of the young spruce tree. This is cooked before being eaten. They use the gum of the spruce tree for chewing, as well as the imported gum. One stick often does service for several members of the family.

One of their most popular vegetables is seaweed. This resembles the cabbage leaf, but is finer, when taken from the sea. There is much labour connected with curing it. It is spread in the sun and just before it is thoroughly dry it is seasoned with cockle juice or the juice of some other shellfish. It is then put into a five-gallon oil can and pressed into square cakes about an inch thick. To accomplish this a layer of seaweed is put in and then a layer of fine hemlock. The twigs separate the layers of seaweed and give it a flavour that the natives like. The can is thus filled to the top and then a heavy weight is put on the whole to make the desired cakes. Every day when the sun shines it is carefully taken out and each layer exposed to the sun to harden. When the sun goes down it is carefully packed away again. This is repeated for a long time before it is properly cured; when finished it will retain its sweetness for months. The cakes

sell for fifty cents each. Sometimes it is broken
up and cooked with oil, forming a sort of salad,
before it is eaten. But the popular way is to
break it off the cakes and eat it without cooking.

The inner bark of the hemlock is treated very
much in the same manner as seaweed, being
pressed into cakes for future use. This is cooked
before eating.

Tea and coffee are popular beverages, but are
not relished without sugar, as the natives are very
fond of sweets.

Flour is used, but mostly to make flapjacks with
plenty of grease. There are few good cooks, and
fewer who can do anything with flour in the line of
pastry cooking. Stewing and boiling are their
principal ways of cooking. Not many have stoves
with ovens, and but little baking is done, nor do
they have eggs, milk, plenty of butter and other
things usually found in the culinary department
of the average white woman.

All things considered, some of them do remarkably well as cooks. We have sat down to meals
entirely cooked and served by native women that
would appeal to the palate of the most fastidious.
We have sat down to banquets given by natives
where everything was appetizing and well served.
At some of these banquets more than two hundred
were seated, showing that they are very capable
when willing to exert themselves.

The more advanced of the native women are
good housekeepers and equal to preparing good
meals.

It must be remembered, however, that most of
them are exceedingly handicapped, as they have
not the facilities for fancy cooking that their white
sisters have.

XII

EXTINCT CUSTOMS

MANY of the customs of the Thlingets, while they strike the average civilized man as peculiar, ludicrous or cruel, are common to most of the uncivilized and semi-civilized tribes of the earth.

In treating of these, we will divide them into three classes—the obsolete, those about to become so, and those that are yet in full sway.

As war was a popular occupation of the nations during the age of Alexander the Great, so it once was with our native Alaskans. Indeed, at one time it was their chief occupation, carried on for spoils, for the love of excitement and for revenge. The warrior's accoutrements were then the most cherished of the Thlinget's possess ns. In times of peace he was largely engaged in making implements of war.

The boldest and most formidable of all the Thlinget tribes were the Chilkats of the north. The fiercest warriors of the country were the Hydahs. These frequently made war on the Thlingets. Tribute was exacted from the weaker tribes of the Thlingets by the stronger ones. Every tribe had to be in a continual state of defence and preparation for war, as they knew not the hour when they would be surprised by some hostile tribe. In some of these encounters there were terrible butcheries. Those who escaped the

knife or club were carried off to become slaves
of the victorious party.

Treachery was regarded as a lawful means by
which to entrap enemies. Surprise, cunning,
treachery and ambush entered more into their
warfare than open valour. Prisoners of war were
either killed or held as slaves. There are certain
spots in the country where prisoners of war were
taken to be killed. Their heads were cut off and
put in a heap. Children taken in war were not
decapitated. The female children were killed in
a manner too revolting to mention.

Strong and healthy captives were reserved and
held as slaves. Their masters had absolute power
over them and could beat them, sell them or kill
them as they pleased.

Many tribes of the Aleuts, who were a meek and
docile people, were decimated by the fierce Thlingets. The weak and abject Stick Indians were
held in fearful terror of them. When the Thlingets entered their country they dictated the prices
for their furs and other commodities. The fearful Sticks yielded to this dictation and were ter-
ribly oppressed by the haughty Thingets.

During the Russian occupation of Alaska, the
Thlingets attacked Russian settlements. Several
of these attacks have gone down into history, notably the massacre of the Russians at Sitka in June,
1802, the attack led by the famous Katlian at Sitka
in the early part of the nineteenth century, the
massacre at Yakutat in 1805, and other minor
conflicts.

Since the American occupation there have been
several battles between the Americans and natives. At least two of these are now recorded
history—one which took place at Sitka on New

Year's day, 1869, and the other at Wrangell on Christmas night, 1869.

The last great stroke of war between tribes of the Thlingets was delivered in 1851. It was a fearful massacre of the Stickeens, or Wrangellites, planned and executed by the great Kok-won-tons of Sitka. The Wrangellites, some time before, had perpetrated a similar massacre on the Sitkans, and the Kok-won-tons struck back in revenge.

The Wrangellites were lured to Sitka. Under the guise of hospitality a great dance was given in their honour. While in the heat of the dance, and handicapped with their dancing costumes on, they were fallen upon and all put to death with knife and club. It was a frightful slaughter, and one that no Thlinget can ever forget.

Since then there have been no tribal wars. There have been some insignificant feuds and family quarrels, but nothing that would merit the name of war. Strictly speaking, none of their killings would merit the name of war, for they made no declarations of war, sent out no challenges, nor did they line up in battle. All of their attacks were planned in secrecy and executed in strategy. Their supreme concern was to take their enemies by surprise and at a disadvantage.

Their fights with the Russians were not without justification. They were oppressed, insulted, maltreated and debauched by these foreigners. They were fairly driven to avenge the wrongs which these ingrates had inflicted upon them. They were peaceably inclined and showed themselves friendly toward the intruders until they saw with what a set of cruel, avaricious and immoral adventurers they had to deal. Then they showed that they did not lack the spirit to avenge their wrongs and defend themselves. As their Caucasian enemies had superior weapons of warfare, in order to gain an advantage they had to resort to strategy and surprise.

Sometimes tribal jealousies brought on conflicts. The tribe defeated in a dancing contest became jealous of the victorious tribe. Slurs and insults followed until a fight was precipitated. Sometimes a dozen or more would fall before the feud was settled. The killing proceeded until those who had fallen on one side were equal in rank to those who had fallen on the other. When they were dancing and potlatching, if one side made one song more than the other it would cause a quarrel which usually ended in a bloody encounter. Frequently on these occasions the most innocent remarks were misconstrued, and then trouble followed. At Kluckwan a chief has in his possession a large basket known as the Mother-of-baskets and a dish (in reality a wooden trough) known as the Worm-dish. The former stands nearly three feet high from the floor and is about two and one-half feet in diameter, while the latter is about thirteen feet long, two feet wide and a foot and one-half deep. This dish is carved out of a solid log and resembles an immense woodworm. These two receptacles have been used from time immemorial for eating contests. They are filled with food, and whichever side eats the contents first wins the contest.

Some years ago a tribe of the Wrangellites had a contest with a tribe of the Chilkats, the former using the Worm-dish and the latter the Mother-of-baskets. On this occasion the former tribe won. This incensed the other tribe, and a bloody fight followed. Several on both sides fell before the fray was ended. These feuds could hardly be dignified by the name of war. They were mere outbursts of passion engendered by jealousy. We hear no more now of this petty kind of warfare.

Until they came into possession of firearms, the war implements of the Thlingets were very crude. Spears, bow and arrows, knives, clubs and stone axes constituted their weapons of warfare. They could make very little headway with these against the muskets and cannon of the white men.

But the battle-flag of the Thlinget has long been furled and the throb of his war-drum unheard. May the one never be unfurled and the other never heard again.

Slavery is another of their obsolete customs. It has not been so many years ago since this obtained with all of its revolting cruelties. It was at the bottom of most of their wars, as they were conducted chiefly to obtain slaves. There are living to-day not a few who were once held as slaves, and some of them are comparatively young. They and their children are still looked down upon by those who had the good fortune never to come within the grasp of slavery.

" A full third of the large population of this coast are slaves of the most helpless and abject description." So writes Bancroft in his " History of Alaska."

While free men and women captured in war were made slaves, many were born into bondage. Slaves were also captured from other tribes. None but the high-caste, however, were allowed to hold slaves, and the chiefs were, as a matter of course, the largest slave-holders.

These wretched men and women were the con-

stant vi.... of c....elty. They were compelled to
do all k.. d.. of menial work, such as getting wood,
making fires, packing dead game, providing fish,
carrying water, paddling canoes and, in short,
every species of drudgery.

The slave was compelled not only to wait on his
master, but on every member of his master's
household. Women slaves did every hand's turn
for their master's daughter. The master was
supposed not to carry so much as a paddle. His
slave had to do this.

Knowing that their lives were in their master's
hands, they were abjectly submissive to every
command and exceedingly careful to give their
lord no offence. There were several events which
demanded the sacrifice of slaves, and no one could
tell when these events would take place. The
erection of a house, the death of the owner, the
death of any member of his household, an unusual
feast, some occurrence to give shame to the
owner, the mere gratification of his vanity, demanded the sacrifice of slaves.

When a chief died, just as he was expiring several slaves were sacrificed near the door of his
house. A chief was drowned in the treacherous
waters of the Taku river. His body was not
recovered, but at the spot where he was drowned
two of his slaves were put to death and their
bodies thrown into the river.

We have seen in the village of Kluckwan a house
where a slave was put into each foundation hole
of its corners for the posts to rest upon. We were
told that this was done to insure a good foundation. When a member of any chief's family was
tattooed, or had an earlobe pierced for rings, the
event was so important that a slave was sacri-

ficed. If a high-caste man was given any great shame, he would sacrifice a slave or two to wipe out the shame. This showed how rich and important he was.

The grandfather of one of our educated young men was a very high-caste man of the Chilkats. He lived at Kluckwan, a renowned old Indian village. His male slaves lived in a house on one side of his and his female slaves in another on the other side. When he died a number of them were butchered and their bodies thrown into the river.

Another middle-aged man has told us that he was an eye-witness to the killing of a beautiful girl slave. After the killing, he saw them put a rope around her neck and then tow her lifeless body out from the shore. When a sufficient distance from the shore the rope was cut and her body sank, a prey to the fishes.

The dead bodies of slaves were always thrown into the bay, sea or river. They were never accorded the honour of burning or burial. Ignominy was their lot in death as well as in life.

Slaves were frequently manumitted. Several events were the occasions of these manumissions. When a slave dressed his master for the dance in the heirlooms of his tribe he was set free. Sometimes through mere vanity of the owner they were given their liberty. The master would then be talked of as a great man.

The writer knew one man who had such love for his daughter that when she gave birth to a son he was so happy that he set free a valuable slave.

So while the poor slave was in constant fear that he might be killed any day, there was also hope that he might be given his liberty. This hope, doubtless, kept him from utter despair, and led him to be cautious and servile when, without it, in desperation he might have defied his master and even killed him.

Slavery, we are happy to say, no longer exists among the Thlingets. It was blotted out, not as the black man's was, with the musket and sword and at the cost of many precious lives, but by the gentle and peaceable means of the Gospel.

At one time cremation was the universal way of disposing of the dead, except of the bodies of slaves, which were thrown into the water, and the remains of shamans, which were embalmed and deposited in deadhouses. The universal custom now is to bury the dead.

When bodies were cremated the ashes were carefully gathered and placed in a box, and the box was then deposited in a deadhouse. Hundreds of these little deadhouses may yet be seen throughout Alaska. Deposited with the box of ashes were many possessions of the deceased, such as clothing, blankets, tools, food, water and other things. These were for his use in the spirit-land.

According to the belief of the natives, burning the dead assured the spirit of the deceased a warm and comfortable place in the spirit-land. As natives are seldom uncomfortable from heat in this life, but often suffer from the cold, they dread the cold far more than they do the heat. Hence a seat near the fire is the seat of honour and pleasure. In the future life their concern is to avoid the cold and to procure a seat near the fire. If burned, the spirits of the other world detect it, and, seeing that the dead has been used to the fire, give him a seat where he may be comfortable.

The chief objection against native cremation of the dead was their barbarous incantations about the funeral pyre. But we should remember that this was an expression of their grief. No people in the world have keener anguish over the loss of loved ones than the natives of Alaska. We have heard wailings from them that would melt the hardest heart to tears.

While there may be one or more cases of existing polygamy to-day, yet it may be truly said that, as a custom, it is a thing of the past. If indulged in at all it is in violation of the public sentiment and life of to-day. In former years it was commonly practised. All early writers about the natives bear testimony to the fact, and the testimony of the natives corroborates the statements of the historians. Since it is no longer countenanced, we feel justified in classing it as obsolete, though a case now and then may be found.

The cruel toughening process is now a thing of the past. In the winter time, in the extreme cold weather, men and boys would go down to the beach and, naked, jump into the ice-cold water. After floundering around in the water, they would jump out and roll in the snow. They would then switch their nude bodies, or have some one do it for them, until the blood would all but break through the skin. Children, who would naturally shrink from this cruel treatment, were compelled to endure it. Youngsters were treated in this way to teach them endurance and make them brave.

It was often practised by their elders from a spirit of vanity. One who was with us for eight years as interpreter, used to tell us how his uncle (he was an orphan) compelled him when a mere child to suffer this cruel treatment. The author has seen youth and young men, with a pair of drawers as their only garment, go into the woods, wading through two or three feet of snow, and bring out a load of wood on their bare backs. This they did to show what they could endure.

We no longer hear of their submitting themselves or their children to this cruel treatment. It was done, of course, from a good motive, but with mistaken judgment. If they had great powers of endurance, then when necessity required it they would not suffer so much as if they had no such powers. And in those times they never knew what they would be called upon to endure.

Infanticide is another of their cruel practices which has fallen into oblivion. A male child has always been a welcome addition to the Thlinget household. But not so a female. In earlier times, when they came too fast, their little lives were strangled. Twins, also, as they were looked upon as an evil omen, were disposed of.

While there may be yet isolated cases of infanticide before birth and with children born out of wedlock, yet as a custom it has passed away. When prevalent no one raised his hand against it. Public opinion was not opposed to it. To-day it is.

The common method of putting little ones to death was to stuff their mouths with moss or grass. This was done by women, generally relatives of the mother. Babes were usually carried to the woods to be put to death.

Tattooing the body was another of their cruel customs which has succumbed to the enlightened principles of truth. Totemic designs were worked in the body and native dyes poured into the punctures and abrasions of the skin. It was a mark of great endurance to submit to this process.

Tattooing was done more from vanity than anything else. It gratified their love of adornment and their boast of endurance. The Thlinget who could not endure bodily pain and suffering without flinching and without a groan was despised.

Gambling, a vice which is still prevalent with the white people, and one which had a tremendous hold on the natives some years ago, is now a back number. This used to absorb most of their time and most of their means. In some instances they gambled away their wives and even themselves. When the latter was done they became the slave of the one who won. More than once the writer has seen circles of native gamblers seated on the beach in the open, gambling for the stakes shining within the ring. It was curious to hear their weird singing and see them beating with sticks at the same time on a pole running horizontally between the players. This was done to divert the attention of the players on the opposite side while the gambling peg was dexterously thrust under the moss in the ring.

Was it the Wolf, the Bear, the Salmon, the Keet, the Eagle, the Crow, etc., which was slipped under the moss? This was the problem. All eyes had been eagerly watching, but who can tell? After some deliberation the fatal guess was made. If correct, the side of the winning party sent up a shout of victory that was heard throughout the village. If the one guessing failed, then there was high glee for the opposite side.

The native gambling pegs were about five inches long and three-eighths of an inch in diameter. They were of uniform size, highly polished, and each was marked differently. There were usually seventy-two in a pack. These pegs were fine specimens of native art. They were all hand-

made and yet as true and perfect as if turned by
a machine. Each was prettily decorated with native colours, and each was named, taking, as a
rule, the name of some animal. The trump, or
leading, stick of the pack was called *nawk* (devil
fish). The player would skilfully conceal this important stick with two or three others in a bunch
of shredded cedar bark or moss. Two of these
bunches would be thrust in front of the opponent,
when he would be required to guess in which bunch
was the *nawk* stick. If he guessed correctly a
count was given in his favour and it became his
turn to shuffle. If he failed he had another trial,
and so on up to a certain number of failures.
Usually the tenth failure lost him the game, but
sometimes it would run to as high as eighteen.

Then, again, the party guessing would name
what sticks were in the bunch of moss. The ones
he named correctly would count so much in his
favour.

This game was at one time the most popular of
gambling games with the natives.

Another similar game was played with two principal sticks, which were short enough to be con-
cealed in the hand, and a number of plain sticks.
One of the two principal sticks was carved while
the other was perfectly plain. The players were
divided into two parties, or opposite sides, but
only one player on each side was allowed to handle
the sticks. This he did very rapidly when the
leader opposite called: " Hands out! " He then
endeavoured to guess which hand held the carved
stick called *nagon*. If he guessed correctly his
side took one of the plain sticks, known as a
counter; if otherwise, his side lost one. The side
that succeeded in getting all of the other side's

counters first won the game and took the stakes.

Other games of lesser interest were played, but were not so popular as the above-mentioned games. In fact, the passion for gambling, which once burned so fiercely in the native's breast, was completely subdued by the influence of the Gospel. The gambling habit has long since passed away and the old gambling devices are seldom seen.

XIII

WANING CUSTOMS

WE pass from the obsolete customs to those which still exist but are waning. Witchcraft, that so long has held terrible sway over the natives, is one of these, but will be treated in another connection.

All were once completely under the spell of this wretched superstition. All sickness and death was attributed to it. Witch-doctors are now few as compared with the number that once thrived, and these are largely discredited. The white man's doctor is now consulted and the native sick are treated in our hospitals. We believe that witchcraft will soon be altogether a thing of the past.

The old marriage system of the Thlingets is giving way to the Christian marriage ceremony, but not a few are yet living together according to the old system.

Marriages are brought about among the natives in more ways than one. Sometimes a youth or young man chooses a girl or woman for himself, frequently scheming relatives determine the match; sometimes marriages are arranged according to the request of the dying, sometimes the levirate custom regulates them, and occasionally headstrong youth defy all customs and marry as they will. Girls seldom have any choice in their own marriage, but act in obedience to the dictates of their relatives and the rules of the people.

Often they do not see the men who are designed to become their husbands until they are wedded to them. There is no such thing as courtship. If a young girl received the attentions of a young man as our girls do, it would shock the natives beyond measure, and would be considered a terrible disgrace. Every girl is carefully watched and restrained from making any approaches to men. Their law of modesty requires that no girl shall speak to a man, not even to her own brother.

When a young man makes his own selection of a girl or woman for a wife, he makes known his desire to his mother, or to a maternal aunt if he has no mother, or perhaps to his sister. He does not approach his sister directly but through her husband. There are no old maids among the natives, nor do widows long remain such. It is considered a disgrace for a girl to remain many months without being married after she becomes a woman. Rarely do they wait at all. So sisters of age usually have husbands, and their brothers use these husbands as mediums of approach when they wish any favour from their sisters who have attained womanhood.

Having made known his desire to any one of these close relatives, that relative reveals the fact to the other close relatives. If they approve of his choice, they interview the girl's people to get their consent. The girl is not consulted at all. If they are high-caste people there is a great deal of palavering about it before it comes to an issue. The youth's relatives (and only those of his mother's totem are considered such, his father and his father's people having nothing to do with it) set forth as strongly as they know how his many good qualities, accomplishments, and his ancestral line.

If the girl's people (those of her mother's totem) regard the proposal of the young man's relatives favourably, they in turn set forth her noble qualities, and accomplishments, and ancestral line, as strongly as they can; and before the palaver is over they tell what they think they ought to have as a dowry. If all are agreed, then the young man is brought, together with the presents that are to be made, to the girl's home. He and the girl then, through the mutual understanding of their recognized relatives, become husband and wife. The presents are given not in the sense of a purchase of the girl, but as the binding feature of the contract. This is to make the union solid, and generally is very effective, especially on the girl's side; for if she proves unfaithful or should run away from her husband, her people must pay back to his people what they gave as a dowry, or its equivalent. This inclines them to encourage and advise the girl to be faithful and to stand by her husband.

If a man casts off his wife, he is not held accountable. The wife goes to her people and little or nothing is done about it. It is considered such a disgrace for a wife to be cast off by a husband that she will endure the most brutal treatment, and sometimes even death itself, before she will leave him.

If the girl's relatives do not approve of her marrying the young man who desires her as a wife, his relatives are so informed. Whether they carry the day or not depends upon the determination of the girl's people. But usually their refusal settles it.

The greatest barriers to marriages are differences in caste and intriguing relatives. No Thlinget parent wants his son or daughter to marry one of a lower caste, nor do relatives approve of it. They oppose this with all of their energy, and such opposition frequently stands in the way of a man who wishes to marry a girl. Relatives who have planned to marry the girl to some one else also block many a man's matrimonial ambition.

The relatives of the girl are very desirous, as a rule, to marry her to some one on the father's side of the family. It may be an uncle, a cousin, or a grandfather. The same principle holds true with the relatives of the young man, who seek to marry him to some girl or woman who is a near relative of his on the father's side. It may be his cousin, or aunt, or grandmother. Such marriages are not only considered very proper among the natives, but they more heartily desire them than marriages of any other connection. In choosing a husband for a girl, relatives consider the young man's accomplishments and his family connections. The man's relatives, in choosing for him, prefer a girl or woman who is modest, industrious and has some accomplishments as a basket-maker, bead-worker, seamstress and housekeeper.

A dying wife sometimes requests that her husband marry a certain girl or woman after she is gone. The motive prompting such a request is usually the desire to keep her personal effects within her own family, the native custom being for the relatives of the survivor to appropriate all of the deceased's belongings, whether husband or wife.

A dying request of this nature is very highly respected and is usually carried out. In one case that came under our notice, a wife died from consumption. Before her death she mentioned a young girl whom she wanted her husband to take as his wife after she was dead. Though the girl lived more than a hundred miles away, and the husband knew very little about her, yet the dying request of the wife was carried out to the letter.

The levirate custom regulates many marriages; that is, when a brother dies some one of his surviving brothers must take his widow to wife. If the deceased left no brother, then the next closest relative of his must make the widow his wife. On the other hand, if the wife dies, then a sister of the deceased, or a close relative, must be given to the surviving husband for a wife. The widow has the right of selection from any of her deceased husband's relatives and the surviving husband has the same right with the relatives of his deceased wife.

It will be seen that this form of marriage among the Thlingets corresponds precisely with that of the ancient Hebrews. It is also interesting to note that there is a correspondence in other respects between the marriage customs of the two peoples; for example, in the dowry, the choice of husband and wife by parents, etc.

It is very common for the nephew of the deceased husband to take his widow to wife, the nephew being considered the nearest relation to a man next to his brother. Also for the niece of the deceased wife to marry the widower, as the niece is the nearest relative of a woman next to her sister.

In levirate marriages no presents are passed

from the man's people to the people of the woman he takes to wife, for this is only making good his loss.

The surviving husband has the right even to select a married sister of his deceased wife. If this is done, she must leave her husband and become the widower's wife. Or the widow has the right to select even a married brother of her deceased husband. And if this is done, the husband must leave his wife and children and become the widow's husband. The writer is acquainted with more cases than one of this kind. A man in our community was suddenly killed. His widow selected one of his married brothers who at the time was living at Sitka. He promptly left his wife and children and came to live with his brother's wife, and they are now living happily together. If a brother should refuse to take to wife his deceased brother's widow he would be disgraced among his people.

If the brother selected by a widow is an old man, a boy is also given to her to be her husband when the old man dies. This system makes some very peculiar matches. We see old men married to girls yet in their teens, and old, wrinkled-faced women married to mere boys.

Little need be said about those who take marriage into their own hands in defiance of all custom. They simply elect to live together and do so, facing the scorn of their people.

Child marriages are by no means uncommon. Boys and girls are mated by their relatives, and infants and mere children are sometimes promised in marriage.

But few marriages are love-matches, but cases of pure love are not altogether wanting. We

knew of a young man who worked for a girl's
parents for years, like Jacob for Rachel, for the
girl he loved. He would kill deer, provide fish,
hunt seal, get wood, and do anything he could for
her parents for the promise that he could have
her at a certain time. The girl loved him. The
parents wanted her to marry another man, an
older and uglier fellow. She absolutely refused
to have him, threatening to be bad if she could not
have the man she wanted. The parents yielded
on condition that the youth of her choice work
for them for a period. This was done, and at the
end of the time the youth took his wife.

The natives have a different standard of beauty
from that of the white people. Beauty, indeed,
cuts little figure with them. The qualities that
count in a girl are caste, then ability to sew or
weave, and then modesty, which leads her to stay
at home and never to speak or look at a man.
To test a girl's modesty when she came from her
little coop of confinement, some one would shout,
" Fire! Fire! " If she paid no attention to the
cry and looked toward the ground, it was considered that she was modest and that she would
make a desirable wife.

A rule which is still in full force, the violation
of which means deep disgrace to the violator and
in earlier times was punished with death, is that
a man must marry a woman outside of his own
totem or totemic phratry.

As soon as the obsequies for the deceased are
over a feast follows. During the progress of the
feast members of the tribe of the deceased ask
the widow which of their tribe she will take for
a new husband. The one whom she mentions becomes her husband.

Another rule closely observed is that no girl shall in any wise propose marriage to a man. If she did she would be held in everlasting disgrace. Nor can any young man approach a girl on the subject. As we have already said, relatives arrange matrimonial matters.

In former years men and women commonly took each other on trial. If, after having lived together for some weeks or months, they found that they liked each other and were satisfied to live together permanently, then, by a mutual understanding, they became husband and wife for good. Only a few years ago we found a man and woman living together in this style. When asked if they were married, he said no, but that they were just living together with the view of marrying providing they liked each other. We did not hesitate to tell them that they were not living right according to the white man's standard of morality.

The old custom of Thlinget marriage is, as we have said, waning, and to-day the Christian marriage ceremony is largely invoked. The author has performed the Christian ceremony for scores of them.

Many white men have taken native women for wives and in most instances have married them according to law. Some of these marriages have been very happy, while others have been anything but happy. Half-breed children are very common in Alaska, many being legitimate.

Not a few are now holding on to the property when either the husband or the wife dies. In nearly every instance, however, they have to fight for it, as the relatives of the deceased claim it. The writer has more than once been called upon to protect property rights for the widow or the widower. It works great hardship on poor natives when widows and orphaned children are stripped entirely of their worldly effects and then thrown on the cold charity of relatives. Sometimes they fare all right, but frequently they suffer from this species of spoliation.

For high-caste natives, especially for chiefs, the erection of totem poles was at one time a common custom. Occasionally one is erected in this day, but this will soon be reckoned as one of the customs of the past.

One of the most curious waning customs is that of confining girls when approaching womanhood in some cramped, coop-like place. Usually this little jail is built by the house with a hole for entrance made in the side of the house. It is very primitive in nature, made out of rough slabs or even of boughs. In one family known to the writer, girls were confined in a pit under the floor of the house, which was entered by a trapdoor. All light is excluded except what may find its way through cracks and through the door when opened. In these little dungeons, not high enough for them to stand in nor long enough for them to stretch out in, girls are confined anywhere from four months to one year. When they come out they are fairly bleached, and the great wonder is that they ever live to come out at all. The places are usually dirty and dank, without light and ventilation, and their inmates are deprived of all means of exercise and fed on a very limited diet. Happily this custom, while yet largely observed, has not the universal sway that it once had, and not a few native girls who come to womanhood to-day are strangers to this ordeal.

This practice advertises to the community that

the girl so confined is of marriageable age and will
soon be ready for matrimonial orders. Indeed,
she is not long out of her little pen before she is
a bride. In most cases she is spoken for before
she leaves her solitary confinement, and she steps
out of her little prison only to step into matri-
mony. The Thlingets may not go all the way with
Josh Billings who says, " Marry early and often,"
but they do go at least half-way with him; for they
believe in early marriages. For them, I am inclined to think that this is good policy. Their
young people settle down, and their girls have a
protector before they go astray and fall down.

XIV

PRESENT-DAY CUSTOMS

THE feast is by far the most popular of all customs, and the one to which they cling most tenaciously. It will probably be the last to pass away.

The " potlatch " (the Chinook term for free gift) and the common, almost perennial, feast of the natives are two different affairs. There is a feast held in connection with the potlatch, but its prime feature is the giving away hundreds of dollars worth of goods by some man who wishes to establish a name for himself among the people.

But potlatches are few as compared with the total number of feasts. They are held to honour the dead, to benefit the dead, to pay off obligations, to wipe out stains on one's reputation, in commemoration of the dead, for self and family glorification, for sociability. So desirous of feasting are they that sometimes they welcome a death, as it affords them an excuse to observe this favourite custom. Where the sick have been expected to die and then have recovered, natives have been known to be greatly disappointed and to regret the recovery, as the feast they anticipated in case of death did not come off. For this reason some are not urgent in employing a doctor when relatives are sick.

A feast must be held whenever a Thlinget dies, whether man, woman or child. It cannot be omitted, as it would be regarded as a woeful lack of respect to the dead and would bring severe reproach on the family.

Besides honouring the dead, the festival has a superstitious significance. It is believed that in some way it actually benefits the dead. For this reason, while the feasting is in progress food is thrown into the fire, and the name of the dead in whose honour the feast is held is called out. The fire-spirit in some way conveys the food to him in the spirit-land. If the feast were omitted, or a poor feast given, the spirit of the dead would feel badly about it and reproach relatives so remiss in their duty. If a good feast is given, then the souls abiding in the spirit-land will treat the departed one with all due respect, as they observe how he is regarded by his people left behind.

At this feast all obligations incurred in the cremation or burial of the dead are met and extravagantly paid for. The higher the rank or caste of the deceased, the more is paid for every service. The natives are not satisfied unless much money is spent, but everything done for the dead is by those of another totem than that of the deceased. The slightest service must be well paid for, and anything given must be returned in value several fold. These are obligations which no Thlinget would think of disregarding, as he would be put to everlasting shame.

The size and expense of the feast depends altogether upon the standing and family connections of the deceased. If one of importance and a high caste dies, nothing short of a great feast will do. Every member of the tribe of the deceased contributes what he can toward it, and there is no giving grudgingly, but cheerfully.

The guests of the feast must be those of a different totem from that of the ones giving the feast. Members of the totem belonging to those giving the feast may attend and look on, but they cannot receive anything.

A feast is usually held immediately after the death of a person, but not always. Death may occur when it is inconvenient for the friends of the deceased to give one at once. They may be too poor, or it may be in the summer time when the people are scattered. But as soon as the relatives of the dead can accumulate the means and the people are back in the village, then the celebration in honour of the memory of the dead must be given.

Frequently a light feast is given by the family right after the obsequies, and in due time a big one follows.

After a period of two or more years another feast may be given in honour of the same person. This is the commemorative feast, and to all intents and purposes is the same as the other.

As soon as convenient after the burial (or cremation) of the body a grave fence (formerly a deadhouse) is erected. This event calls for a feast, given primarily to pay off those who had any hand in erecting it. In course of time a suitable monument is set up in memory of the dead. This again calls for a feast, at which those who assisted in setting it up are paid for their services.

The completion of certain masks used by chiefs in dancing, the building of a canoe, the erection of a totem, and of a house, calls for a feast, the primary purpose being to pay those who did the work.

These items are tribal property, and all tribal

property must be made, built or erected by those of another tribe than the one owning them.

This is the process of Thlinget settlement. They are perfectly satisfied with this method, though they must wait months or even years before a feast can be given and a settlement effected. While they do not keep books, yet every one remembers accurately what is due him until he has been paid, no matter how long the settlement is put off. The women, especially, keep tab on every one under any obligations to their families.

It often happens that when a man completes his house he has no money with which to make a feast and meet his obligations. His creditors are content to wait until such time as he can give it.

This system has made them poor debtors so far as the white man is concerned. To delay to pay an honest debt to the white man seems nothing to them. The truth is that too many of them are unscrupulous in this respect, and will not pay their debts to a white man if they can get out of it. They cannot very well shirk this duty among themselves, as every debtor is hounded until he or his tribe pays.

The events which call for feasting for self and family glorification are the erection of totem poles, piercing the ears and nose for rings, naming a child, tattooing the person, and when a girl becomes a woman. The feast for any of these occasions proclaims to the community the high standing of the one giving it and his family. So the Thlinget aristocrats have their way of publishing to the world their social status as well as those of Gotham.

CHILKAT POTLATCH DANCING.

Feasts are sometimes given to whitewash a disreputable character. If a man has disgraced himself in the eyes of his people, he may give a generous feast, and no one after that is allowed to mention or talk about his dishonourable conduct. Giving a feast wipes out the stain, and the sinner may hold his head as high as ever, knowing that he is not talked about as he was before he gave the feast, as that put a quietus on gossip.

In the settlement of all feuds, insults, serious quarrels and the cutting of a child, feasts must be given. When a child has been cut the parents believe the scar does not look so bad as it would if no feast had been given. This is a wonderful balm to the wounded sensibilities of the Thlinget.

The death of a chief, shaman or very high-caste man calls for a very large and expensive feast. It is attended by men, women and children. Generally the room in which it is held is one solid mass of humanity. In some feasts they squat on the floor in family groups. There is one large bowl to the group, generally a wash-bowl, which may hold anything in the nature of liquid food, a stew, or boiled meats, or fish. All in the group help themselves from this common bowl with a spoon or fingers. Food like pilot bread, crackers, apples, etc., is dumped on a cloth on the floor or held in the lap. The head of the family circle takes with her to the feast a flour sack or pillow slip. After all have eaten what they can they put what is left into this sack and carry it home. Such is the generosity at these feasts that the guests cannot begin to consume all the food that is distributed. Liquid food, such as oils and berries in oil, they carry home in their bowls or kettles.

In some feasts the people are seated in divisions. This is especially true when dancing is held in connection with them. During their progress, in many instances, speech-making is indulged in and there is much merriment. On these occasions legends are rehearsed and exploits recounted. By the time a Thlinget becomes a man he has heard the legends of his people over and over again.

Fasting may precede feasting—not to enable them to eat more, but to bring good luck to all who partake of the feast. The Thlinget's superstition leads him to believe that there are many things he can do which will insure him good luck. Many white people are not far behind him in this.

It is a common practice for them to say one thing and mean another. The Thlingets are experts in handling innuendo, and no less so in perceiving the hit that is conveyed in the same. In truth they are a little too sensitive at times, taking offence where none is intended. This has frequently been the case in religious services conducted by missionaries. On one occasion a lame native got up in the midst of a service and left the church, offended because the preacher read in the Bible about the " lame and the halt." He said it was calling attention to his infirmity and he resented it.

The potlatch is given primarily for self-glorification. The man who gives one receives honour and public esteem for himself and his family in proportion to the amount he gives away. He is the most renowned who has given the greatest or the greatest number of potlatches. A man who is ambitious to give a potlatch will save and stint

for years, even to the extent of denying himself
and family the necessities of life, that he may give
as big a one as possible. The members of his
family contribute their quota and endure the pri-
vations it entails. From two to five thousand dollars worth of goods are sometimes given away in
a single potlatch. Men absolutely impoverish
themselves and families, but their poverty is pa-
tiently endured for the name that has been established. Henceforth the man is an honoured member of the community, however low he was before
he gave the potlatch. He and his will be given
a seat of honour in all public functions and a
liberal share of what is distributed in every feast
to which they are invited.

Feasting and dancing are important features of
the event and are never omitted.

Invitations to attend a potlatch are sent by
special messengers long before the affair is to
come off; sometimes the people know of it months
or even years before it takes place. Men, women
and children attend, as at all their feasts. Invitations are sent to the people of distant villages and
to those of a different phratry from the one to
which the man giving the potlatch belongs. Those
of the great man's totem may attend, but they
cannot receive any of the gifts that are distributed. The wife of any man or the husband of
any woman who is of the same totem as the one
giving the potlatch may and does receive gifts,
as the totem is different from that of the native
philanthropist.

When the important day comes, the village is a
whirl of intense excitement. The honoured guests,
two hundred or more in number, are sighted as
they approach in their canoes. Flags wave from

the prow and stern of every canoe and on the shore. Before a canoe of the happy fleet touches the strand, they are drawn up in peaceful array to hear words of welcome from the great chief. After the response from the spokesman of the incoming guests, they all draw to the shore and their hospitable friends receive them to their homes.

For the next week or ten days things are moving in this village. Every day and night feasting and dancing engage and thrill the merry-makers. The great tribal heirlooms are brought out and totemic emblems are profusely displayed on paraphernalia of every description. Faces are painted with stripes betokening the totem of the individual wearing them. Now we see a Crow, now an Eagle, now a Bear, now a Frog. What gorgeous costumes some wear! What ludicrous ones have others! Here comes a bear! But no; it is only a man in a bear's skin. Look at that mammoth crow! But it is not a real crow. It is only a man under a great mask to represent the doleful bird. The dull, monotonous beat of the drum is frequently heard—the only object resembling a musical instrument used in the potlatch; doleful as it is, it excites the natives who hear it. The communal house where the great potlatch is given is thronged and is the scene of varied activities. The dancers take their places, and after an appointed spokesman has made some appropriate remarks, dancing begins. After this set has danced an hour or more, a fresh set from another tribe takes the floor. Feasting is interspersed and the distribution of the goods to be given away is made. Great bundles of blankets, prints, muslin and edibles of various kinds are given out. While many of the blankets are given away whole, others are torn into quarters and these fractions are bestowed. The prints and bolts of muslin are given out by the yard, the edibles in quantity. Every man receives according to his social standing. While the dancing is in progress various songs peculiar to the tribe of the one giving the potlatch are sung, or, more correctly speaking, chanted.

The period covered in giving a potlatch varies according to the amount of goods which have been accumulated to be given away. It may be from one to six days. It often happens, however, that several are ready to give potlatches in succession, and so they run along without a break for two or three weeks.

The potlatch is conducted according to well-defined rules laid down by custom, and no departure from these rules is tolerated.

Dancing.—While dancing is usually held in connection with feasting and potlatching, yet we need to distinguish it from these. Feasts are often held without dancing and dancing without feasting.

The native dance is very different from the white man's. It is practically a charade, an imitation, or representation, of the chief characteristics of some totemic animal, as the bear, crow or whale.

There are several different dances and each is known by its own name, and has its own particular features. Among the more important ones are the War Dance, the Peace Dance, the Ptarmigan Dance, the Tsimpshean Dance and the Stick Dance.

The dancers are divided into bands, each from some distinctive tribe. Only one band dances at a time, and when they have played their part they give way to one from another tribe. They dance in rivalry and frequently engender envy, jealousy, contention and strife. Each side watches carefully its opponents and notices and remembers the slightest mistake made while dancing, or any remark which they can construe as a slur. Anything which can be considered a reflection on dancing or persons is eagerly seized upon and made the basis of a quarrel.

While dancing, the participants stand close together and scarcely move out of their tracks. They are surrounded, as a rule, by a large body of spectators, who confine them in a positive area. The dancing really consists of rhythmic movements of the hands, arms, head and entire body above the waist. To the white spectator, some of these motions are extremely ludicrous and laughter-provoking; but to the native it is serious business and he wears a sober countenance through it all. Time is measured by the beat of the drum—now soft, now loud, now slow and now rapid, and by the incessant chant of females from start to finish. All movements are in harmony with the time thus measured.

The dance is highly spectacular and dramatic. Striking and singular costumes are worn, some of which are highly valued. Tribal heirlooms in the way of wooden hats, masks, ear-drops, headgear, robes, batons, etc., which have been handed down from generation to generation, are much in evidence. The participants are men, women and children. Their faces are streaked with paint, red or black, rings are in their noses and ear-drops in their ears. Some of the leading actors wear headpieces with flexible projections six or eight inches long sticking out of the top. These

prongs are filled between with eagle's down, and
every once in awhile during the dance the proud
wearer of this peculiar headgear gives his head a
terrific shake, sending the down flying through
the air like a snowstorm. Thus, all tricked out
in their various trappings and finery, they dance
to their hearts' content. One dance often occupies hours.

The writer has witnessed a number of native
dances. The largest, most spectacular and most
significant of these was at a place called Angoon,
a village belonging to the famous Hootz-na-hoos.
On this occasion bands from the Hootz-na-hoos
and from some of the leading tribes of Sitka performed. The dance, which was held in connection
with a big potlatch, took several days, and the
Sitka bands walked off with the honours and with
a cargo of the spoils from the potlatch. The star
dancer of the Sitkans, however, lost her heart to
one of the young lords of the Hootz-na-hoos and
she became his wife. So the Hootz-na-hoos had
at least some compensation for their lavish enter-
tainment of the Sitkans. This big dance was carried through in a harmonious spirit, and was such
as no white man will probably ever look upon
again.

Other minor prevalent customs require only
brief reference.

The absurd custom of brothers and sisters (as
soon as the latter attain to womanhood), the
mother-in-law and son-in-law, males and females
of the same totem, refraining from speaking to
each other, still finds favour with many. The
writer has known sisters who, on their return to
Alaska, after being away to school in the States,
could not get their uneducated brothers to speak

to them. A nephew, who had been educated in one of our schools, made repeated efforts to get his aunt to speak to him while on a long journey, but failed. The untutored aunt would not condescend to speak to her nephew, as it was contrary to her notions of womanly modesty and ethics. It is considered improper for a brother and sister to sit in the same room if no others are there. A brother refused to enter the church until the arrival of others because his sister was the only one inside. A brother may not make a present to his married sister, but may to her husband. It is considered highly improper for a brother to give his married sister anything.

The Thlingets would sooner sustain great personal loss than face the opprobrium which would be heaped upon them for the violation of any popular custom. Public scorn is the most dreaded thing imaginable to them. And nothing invites it like the violation of their customs.

XV

THE DISPOSITION OF THE DEAD

NO event with the Thlingets involves so much as death. It sets many curious customs in motion, all being dependent on the rank and class of the deceased. If a chief, great lamentation is heard from the entire tribe. As soon as he expires messengers are sent all over the country to announce his death to his tribal relations. No matter how far away they may be at the time, no disposition is made of the body until they arrive. It lies in state, clothed in the very best of garments. The most costly blankets and robes of his tribe are brought out, wrapped around and thrown over him. The old tribal heirlooms are placed on top of his coffin. His weapons of warfare, the instruments he used in hunting, and house-totems are placed beside him. In the days of cremation his totemic marks were painted in red on his face. These things reveal to any who enter the house the high standing and connections of the man in life.

The body properly placed in state, the widow takes her place on the floor beside the body, not to leave the spot until the remains are removed for burial. Her robe is a coarse blanket, a token of bereavement. Most of the time she lies hunched up, and as silent as the corpse beside her. Her hair is shorn and her face painted black all over, in token of mourning. Hired mourners take their places also beside the remains. All mourners must be of an opposite tribe from that of the deceased.

These particulars properly carried out, attention is turned toward collecting things for the great feast which must follow. The first step toward this is to collect all the money possible from the members of the dead man's tribe. All are loyal in giving and no trouble is had in raising the money needed for the feast. It would be great shame to one not to give. The stigma would cling to him for a long time.

Boxes of pilot bread, apples, canned goods and other foods are purchased, and to these are added home food products such as dried fish, fish oil and various kinds of berries preserved in fish oil.

While the food is being collected for the feast by some, others are busy digging the grave which, in the case of the burial of a chief, must be lined with suitable lumber.

As soon as the distant relatives of the deceased arrive, the officiating missionary is sent for, if a Christian service is to be held in the home. Frequently funeral services are held in the church. The ceremony over at the home or the church, hired pallbearers convey the casket to the hearse or to the burial ground. In these days a band of music often plays dirges and funeral marches as the procession moves along. Women have gathered up all the articles intended to be buried with the body, and taken them to the grave. The brief ceremony there being over, the mourners sit with their backs to the grave and give vent to real or assumed grief.

Often the whole ceremony is delayed for the men to enlarge the grave to accommodate the

All
hat

en-
the
tep
ble
All
ng
eat
ng

nd
ed
ad

st
h,
d

d
a
e-
l.
l,
e
f
s
-
l
e
e
e
e

coffin or while they make the box for it. The grave-diggers are so averse to throwing one shovelful of earth more than is absolutely necessary that the hole is usually too small for the coffin and the grave must be enlarged.

Articles of clothing and bedding (and if for a child, playthings), and always a vessel of water, are buried beside the coffin. Sewing-machines, clocks, guns and various other articles such as were used and prized in life are often deposited on the grave.

The funeral over, the guests repair to the house where the all-important feast is to be given. This has a threefold purpose: to honour the memory of the dead, to feed his spirit as it travels to the spirit-land and to pay off all who have any claim on the family of the deceased for any services rendered in their bereavement.

As the dying must be dressed for burial before life has departed from the body, all who assisted in that put in a claim. The natives think it is terrible if the dying are not dressed for the tomb before life leaves the body. This is to avoid touching the dead, of which they have a superstitious fear. We have seen men with their burial clothes on two or three days before death. It does not disturb the mind of a dying native thus to dress him, or even to bring his coffin into his presence before he passes away. In fact most of them prefer to see these things before they die. They have no fear of death, and most of them face it as calmly as if lying down to sleep.

All who contributed anything, and the pall-bearers, coffin-box builders, grave-diggers, etc., must be liberally remunerated.

By the time the various claims and the other

expenses have been met two or three hundrē
dollars have been swallowed up, but every penny
of this is cheerfully paid, as it would be a deep
disgrace to refuse any of these claims. But the
expenses connected with the dead do not end here.
As soon as possible a grave fence and a tombstone
must be erected. These must be as good as money
can buy. Often expensive monuments are bought.
They must be conveyed to the burial ground and
set up by those of an opposite tribe from that of
the dead. This requires a feast when those who
erected them are paid.

The disposition of the bodies of those not so
high in rank as chiefs, and of the common people
other than slaves (whose bodies were cast into
the sea), is similar to that of chiefs, only not so
imposing and expensive. But no matter how poor
a family, they strain every point to give their dead
expensive burial.

In the days of cremation, the ashes, and the
bones of the dead not completely burned, were
carefully collected, put into a sack made of cloth,
and the sack deposited in a box which was kept
in the family deadhouse. The bones of each were
distinguished from the others by the colour of the
sacks.

The Thlingets are especially fond of giving
feasts for the dead. They will even exhume bodies
and bones to bury them in some other spot in
order to have an excuse for such feasting. In
one instance two relatives had a serious quarrel
as to which one should have the privilege of taking
the bones of a deceased relative from a deadhouse
to bury them. One of them became so angered
that he took the bones and scattered them in the
bushes. The members of an opposite totem had

to be hired to collect them, and they were finally buried with great pomp.

Feasts are frequently given in commemoration of the dead. A son will do this for his deceased mother, a brother for a brother, or a nephew for an uncle. It may be in honour of one who has been dead a number of years.

In the days of cremation, and even later, dead bodies were never taken through the door, but through a hole made in the side of the house and then closed up so that the spirit of the deceased could not find its way back into the house. Or the body was taken through the aperture in the roof and a dog taken along with it. If the dog were not taken they believed that some one of the family would surely die, but if the spirit of the deceased entered the dog it would not return to the injury of any member of the household.

With an occasional exception in the case of children, the dead are never buried from the house in which they die, but are taken to some other house belonging to one of the same tribe.

From the moment of death until the body is disposed of, some one must remain with the corpse day and night and a light must burn every night. This is to guard against the intrusion of spirits. The Greek church custom of burning candles about the dead appeals strongly to this phase of their superstition and conforms to their practice.

Down to the present generation embalming was practised. Mummies have been found in Alaska, some of which may now be seen in the Smithsonian Institute. The universal custom now is to bury the dead, and they usually hold a solemn funeral service. But more than once we have had the hour set for the service and when we went to hold it have found that they had already gone to the cemetery. They became impatient to get to feasting, and so went without notice to the officiating minister.

Deadhouses are small houses about six by eight by eight. Most bodies are buried in the community burial ground, or the remains of the deceased are left to repose in a deadhouse within the common deadhouse plot. Occasionally one prefers to bury his relative in some isolated spot, and small islands are selected for this purpose. The bodies of medicine-men are always placed on some high and almost inaccessible promontory. Many a shaman's deadhouse may be seen from the deck of steamers, standing like some grim sentinel fifty, or a hundred, or even two hundred feet above the water. In many instances the canoe of the departed doctor may be seen beside the deadhouse rotting in conjunction with the bones of its owner.

Sometimes the ashes and bones of the dead were deposited in hollow mortuary poles. A number of these poles may yet be seen in the country, although the custom of erecting them is now practically a thing of the past.

Widows painted their faces black as a sign of mourning. If a widow's face was streaked from flowing tears, people pitied her, as they believed she truly missed her husband. But if no such streaks were visible they disliked her and talked about her, believing that she did not care for her husband. Sometimes the living shaved their heads as a sign of mourning, and widows cut their hair.

Songs were introduced at burials to let those in attendance know something of the history of the dead and his family connections.

This was in earlier times, however, and is not practised now. As Christian burial has supplanted cremation, and as Christian rites are largely employed in the final disposition of the body, Christian songs are sung at their funerals. Those in attendance at funerals are always very reverential. But those employed to carry the coffin, place it in the tomb, etc., do not do it with that nice delicacy that white people do. Oftentimes they build and nail up the box that contains the coffin after the funeral procession has arrived at the grave and the bereaved, as well as others in attendance, are compelled to listen to the pounding and sawing until it is completed.

But, they are making progress, and doubtless some day they will be more considerate and careful.

XVI

SHAMANISM AND SUPERSTITIONS

THE part that superstition has played, and still plays, in human affairs is by no means small. It is a child of ignorance and thrives best in the barbarous mind, and yet enlightened people are not altogether free from it.

Belief in witchcraft has ever been the dominant superstition of uncivilized people, and no other superstition has been so prolific of cruelty among men.

While it does not hold the sway over the natives of Alaska that it did some years ago, and while some have thrown it off altogether, yet it is still potent with the mass of the people. Diseases, especially those of a lingering and wasting nature, like consumption, are regarded as the work of malevolent witches.

In former years all sickness and death were attributed to them. This being the case, the only remedy they could think of was to expel the evil spirit that possessed the sick and was doing the mischief. They must either do that or locate and kill the witch. This was regarded as a sacred duty.

For this purpose there were professional men among them known as *ikt*, in their tongue, and called in the English language, medicine-men, Indian doctors and shamans, the last term having been borrowed from the Russians. They were

never very numerous, usually not more than one
or two to a community. Some communities had
none. The friends of the sick in such villages
sent abroad for the *ikt* when needed.

Like our own physicians, some had the reputation of being more skilful in their art than others,
and these enjoyed a larger practice than their less
favoured brethren.

The office of shaman may be inherited, like the
ancient priesthood, but not necessarily so. As a
rule, one must be consecrated to the office from
infancy, and no comb, scissors or water must ever
touch his hair. The longer and more matted the
hair the greater the power the doctor is supposed
to possess. For this reason the hair of an *ikt* was
jealously guarded. If shorn of it his power van-
ished, and he was no longer consulted as a doctor.

The total neglect of the hair was not the only
habit peculiar to this profession. They spent long
periods in the forest in absolute solitude, supposedly in communication with evil spirits. They
also had periods of fasting, and their diet differed in many respects from that of others. They
ate the bark of devilclub and portions of bodies
of the dead. They also procured and held in the
mouth the finger of a dead *ikt*. Just before they
engaged in exorcising evil spirits from the sick,
or in determining who was the witch, they drank
native red paint. They always kept the box containing their paraphernalia on top of the house.
A hot fire was required when performing about
the sick, and they began the ceremony in perfect
nudity. As they warmed to their work, a girdle
composed of bones, claw-nails and talons was put
about their loins, then a necklace of such about
their necks, and last of all they were given rattles

especially made for their use. It was firmly believed that the evil spirits could not be conjured with any other objects than the drum and the rattle.

As the natives felt that good spirits would never harm them, their chief concern was to propitiate the evil ones so they would not.

In case the sick recovered, no witch was hunted. On the other hand, if the patient grew worse and showed signs of dying, then the wily doctor evaded responsibility by asserting that a witch was hindering his work and must be found and killed. For the service of locating the witch, he had to be paid a much larger fee than for merely making one well.

The one settled on as the witch was generally some unimportant member of the community, an uncanny-looking creature, a slave, or some one who had the ill will of the doctor or the relatives of the patient. This was a very effective way of ridding one of his enemy.

No one, not even the victim himself, thought of disputing the shaman's judgment. Whom he designated as the witch was believed by all to be such, and was immediately treated as such. A near relative of the witch usually took the initiative in the punishment.

The victim was first reviled, reproached, brutally and shamefully treated, and subsequently put to death. No punishment was considered too cruel for a witch, and various means were devised for their torture. They were tied to stakes before the rising tide, and to stakes in the forests for wolves to devour; they were made to die from starvation, with food almost within their reach; their limbs were tied to their bodies and then they were

TOTEM POLE

thrown naked on a bed of thorns. In short, all kinds of exquisite tortures were applied to the miserable wretches.

After the witch was left to die, no one would dare approach him, or in any way offer relief. The curse of the community would be on the head of the one who did.

If a witch had the good fortune to escape death, he was shunned by all, and no matter how much he might be in need of assistance, no one would help him. The case of a poor old blind man comes to mind. In his earlier days he had been tied up as a witch, but was rescued from his horrible condition by some white men. To keep him from starving, after he became practically helpless, the white people living about him supported him through charity. No native would do anything for him because he had once been declared a witch by their infallible *ikt*.

It would be almost impossible to exaggerate the native's terror of witches. It is for this reason rather than for hardness of heart or delight in human sufferings, that they torture them. They deem nothing too cruel for them because they hold them responsible for all human sufferings and death itself.

Any one who accuses another of being a witch runs the risk of losing his life at the hands of the accused, or his relatives, for it is deemed such a terrible charge. Even venerated shamans have been killed for this.

A young girl was tied up and after severe torture was compelled to admit that she had made witch-medicine. She was then compelled to dive down and bury the concoction in the bed of the river, the natives believing that if this is done the bewitched will get well. The girl claimed that a certain man taught her to make the fearful medicine. She is now a woman about thirty-five years of age and well known in Alaska.

A boy of a lively and mischievous nature was condemned as a witch. He was spirited away and left to starve in a garret, but the missionary of the place, hearing of the lad's misfortune, rescued him, and sent him to the mission-training school at Sitka. He is there yet and is a youth of promise. This institution has been the refuge of more than one native child who was condemned to die as a witch.

Witch-medicine is composed of several ingredients, such as hair and finger parings of the dead, herbs, and the tongues of birds, frogs and mice. If a native is seen loitering around a native burial ground, he is suspected of being after materials for witch-medicine.

Some, charged with being witches, take a kind of pride in admitting it. They not only glory in making others believe that they have such demoniacal powers, but do it in order to make others fear them.

When witchcraft was in its flower, the *ikt* was superstitiously regarded as an all-powerful being. His word was absolute, and he was revered as a god. All kinds of superstitions were held in connection with him. Fetishes were made of his things. When natives passed his deadhouse in their canoes they threw tobacco or food, such as he had liked in life, into the water to propitiate his spirit, and even prayed to his spirit for a safe journey and success in their hunting ventures. It was also thought disrespectful to pass the spot afar off as if afraid of it. Yet on land no native would venture near the deadhouse of an *ikt*. All berries growing in the neighbourhood of the gruesome tomb were superstitiously eschewed, as it was the universal belief that those who ate such berries would surely die. They were regarded as belonging to the *yak* (spirit) of the dead doctor.

A shaman was never cremated. His body was embalmed, then wrapped in a mat made of basket material, tied securely and then placed in the deadhouse. Things that he owned and prized in life were deposited with him. No matter how costly, they were never in any danger of being stolen, for the tomb of a shaman was regarded as especially sacred. No tomb, however, was ever in danger of being rifled by a native.

When he failed to cure the sick, it was generally believed that he had been too familiar with some woman, and for this reason his all-powerful *yak* had forsaken him.

When eating halibut, no one would pass in front of his door if he knew it. Some one was stationed in front of his door when his highness was thus engaged, and any one about to pass was warned and directed to pass around the back of the house.

The *ikt* was considered not only to be in league and to have influence with evil spirits, but to be a prophet. As such he was often consulted as to weather, the proper time to start on the hunt, whether a certain venture would meet with success or failure and about other things. He would predict epidemics, deaths and other catastrophes. He was considered also to have the gift of tongues. It was believed, for instance, that a Thlinget shaman could speak the Tsimpshean tongue when the Tsimpshean spirit came upon him, but not otherwise.

They were very jealous of one another, discrediting one another, and doing what they could to break down each other's reputation. When jealous, it was said that their spirits were fighting one another.

When in the full swing of his performance, the *ikt* makes such a hideous noise that no spirit, however malignant, is considered to be bold enough to remain in a patient's body. In appearance he is the most diabolical and repulsive-looking of all creatures, and it is scarcely to be wondered at that he fills others with awe and fear.

In this connection we submit an excellent pen picture of one in action, taken from the realistic novel of Mrs. Eugene S. Willard, "Kindashon's Wife."

" Three parts of the great house are filled with people—men, women and children, sitting and standing, densely massed. On the fourth side, opposite the door, with head toward the wall, lies the body of the sick chief; at either end of this long space hang the rewards, and between them is the dancing ground of the doctor, who now sits, limply, near the sick man's feet, with the rattle in his hand.

" He has closed his eyes, and now he begins to breathe more heavily and irregularly—the drum is but touched as by his breath.

" Presently the breathing itself assumes a form of sound; there is a mutter—a rumble, gradually gaining the punctuation of a chant, weird and wild as the cries of a lost soul.

" Now the eyes roll—the sight turns inward, then out again, throwing light lurid as from hell. The muscles begin to twitch, the limbs to jerk, the body to rock and sway as if moved by infernal machinery.

" The sight becomes fixed as held by awful power—the breath comes in snorts—the chant grows louder—the drums beat quick and low; every muscle freezes tense—the air is palpitating with the powers of the unseen world.

" There is a crouching of the visible champion. And now with the cry and spring of a panther he is at the side of the mangled, prostrate form— the chant is now a shriek; the drum-beats indicate the close and awful contact of the opposing forces, the rattle is held aloft and shaken with ferocious vehemence. Now he retreats, crouches, springs clear over the body—wilder and wilder grow the singing and the drum—he writhes as in torment— he shrieks and moans and beats his own body—he leaps into the air with uplifted arms and a blood-curdling yell—there! he has fallen and relapsed into his first position. The sounds have fallen— muffled, also. There is a clutching—a clawing at the invisible—a hissing, with lips compressed, with jaws set; the spitting of a wildcat, the snap and snarl of a maddened dog.

" Palsy seizes the whole frame of the creature, with muscles drawn to tenseness like iron and moved with irresistible power, till, foaming at the mouth, the eyes rolling as in horrible agony, he falls under the power of the spirits he has dared to encounter. Two men spring forward and take him in their grasp, trying to prevent him from eating his own flesh.

" He is now left to himself—for in this swoon are revealed to him the human agencies which are in league with the spirits he has assailed. Woe to the man, woman or child who may have crossed this wretch's will at any time, or to those who are objects of dislike to those rich enough to pay this creature for condemning them!

" The waiting people hold their breath in silence which grows more terrible, not knowing who may be the victim of this consultation with the powers of darkness.

.   .   .   .

" But now the sorcerer moves, twitches and quivers again, and with the seeming agonies of a horrible death he struggles back to human life. Like one muttering in his sleep he speaks—every ear is strained to catch the words which come gurgling from that world of horrors and of mystery:

" ' The spirit of the great chief must pass before us ere the setting of the sun; ' then in the same sepulchral tone comes the name ' Sha-hehe.' What else the sorcerer says and does are lost in the quick, sharp cry of terror from Sha-hehe, and the general hubbub which ensues."

Native superstition is by no means confined to witchcraft. It has a wide range and is a big factor in his life.

His belief in the existence of evil and malignant spirits is the foundation for his belief in witchcraft. He regards them as not only capable of producing disease, but of sending other calamities. They may make a heavy storm swamp his canoe, cause him to be drowned, to be destroyed by bears, triumphed over by his foes, and in other ways do him untold harm.

Many things are regarded by him as evil omens. The birth of twins is one. In former years a man felt justified in leaving his wife if she pre-

are
this

si-
who
the

and
of
ife.
ery
me
ys-

be-
the
le.'
in
nd

to
or

nt
h-
of
ni-
is
ed
er

s.
a
e-

sented him with twins, and she was looked upon by all as something uncanny. Twins were also put to death. In this age they are accepted as a matter of course.

A widow must not eat boiled fish lest her head should loosen and shake from side to side. If the sick suddenly finds a bug on his person, it is regarded as a sign that he will surely die from that sickness.

The aurora borealis is regarded as an evil omen. It indicates that some one will be killed. It is believed that only people who have been killed go up into the sky, the common future home of spirits being some imaginary remote locality beyond the most distant mountains, and inaccessible except through death. When, therefore, the aurora is seen, it is believed that those who have passed to the skies are dancing for joy because some one will be killed and join their number. In former years, when tribal wars were rife, it was considered the sure sign of an approaching battle.

Children are forbidden to throw scraps of food into the water, as the water-dog will get them and then the children will have bad luck; to pick up shells on the seashore will bring a terrific storm.

Charms are worn to ward off evil, and certain things are kept to bring good luck. A woman has kept for years a lot of halibut bones taken from a halibut that was mysteriously caught by a native. The old woman would not part with these bones for anything. A red-bird is kept by a man who caught it while sitting on a log. He has had it for years, and he attributes every piece of good fortune to his possession of this bird. Another is keeping some pretty eggs that he found in a

MICROCOPY RESOLUTION TEST CHART

(ANSI and ISO TEST CHART No. 2)

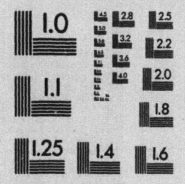

APPLIED IMAGE Inc

1653 East Main Street
Rochester, New York   14609   USA
(716) 482 - 0300 - Phone
(716) 288 - 5989 - Fax

peculiar place, and every turn of good fortune is at once accredited to these eggs.

The tongues of birds and of mice, after having been dried on the top of a house, are considered very potent talismans.

Many natives are firm believers in love-potions. These are made of the tongues of birds, frogs and mice, and of herbs, and the medicine or charm is known as *kă-gä′nē-ē-thloot* (tongue medicine).

When a woman becomes infatuated with a man and her love is not reciprocated, or if a wife observes that her husband's affection is cooling and she wishes to retain it, she resorts to the love-potion. This is made of the ingredients mentioned above and in great secrecy. It is then wrapped in a piece of the loved one's necktie, or shirt, or some other garment, and carefully hidden away, the woman taking good care not to forget the spot where it is hidden, as it is believed if the place is forgotten not only will the potion lose its efficacy, but the woman will also lose her mind.

If this process of winning or retaining the affections is faithfully carried out, it is firmly believed to result in victory. The process, however, of compounding the ingredients in rightful proportions is known to but few. The potion may be bought, but is very costly. This same philter is sometimes resorted to to make one successful in the hunt, dance, witchcraft and in other affairs of life.

It is believed that all animals understand human speech. For this reason natives are careful what they say about them not only in their presence, but at any time; for they have some mysterious way of hearing all said about them, and if evil or boastful things are said, the creature maligned is sure to take offence, and in time will surely harm the speaker. A young man who was subject to epileptic fits, while in one of them fell off the deck of a boat and was drowned. It was said that when he was a child he spoke unkindly to some little fishes, and this was his punishment for it. A young man swore at some mountain sheep which he was hunting because they were in a difficult place to reach. In his effort to reach them a snowslide came down and buried him and he perished. The natives believe that he met with this death because he was disrespectful to the sheep.

When the grampus is seen, he is practically prayed to to bring them good luck. This marine monster feeds on seals, and is generally on the hunt for them. He may direct the hunter to where seals are, so he is graciously addressed when seen.

Even the little *oolikan* are respectfully spoken to; if not, they are supposed to resent it, disappear and, in some way, bring trouble to those who have been so disrespectful.

The crow, raven and eagle, being totemic birds, are never molested by those of their totem.

It is believed that the spirit of the drowned is caught by the land-otter and dragged into his hole, and there it is turned into a "*goosh-ta-kah,*" the native hobgoblin, or ghost of the woods.

On account of this superstition, drowning is considered the worst calamity that can befall one, especially if the body is not recovered. Consequently when a native is drowned diligent search is made to recover his body, heavy rewards are offered and searching parties formed. When Chief Kin-da-goosh was drowned in the Chilkat river the whole country was in commotion, and the river was fairly covered with canoes in which were hundreds of natives looking for his body. The search was maintained until the body was recovered, though it took days to find it. Great would have been their sorrow had the body not been found.

When a husband goes hunting or fishing his wife must not bathe, comb her hair nor look into a mirror, lest it bring him bad luck.

When a woman is pregnant, neither she nor her husband must eat thimbleberries or strawberries.

There are several superstitions in connection with births. A babe must not be born in the house for fear of bringing evil upon it. When delivery is expected the mother moves out and occupies a booth of boughs, or a tent. She must not be touched, as she is considered unclean.

The superstitious belief in the reality and truth of dreams has tremendous hold on the native mind. If a sick native dreams of one bewitching him, that one is positively regarded as a witch. If a husband dreams that his wife has been untrue to him, he believes that she has and gives her a sound whipping on the strength of it.

A woman dreamed that she was struck in the chest by another woman. When she awoke there was a pain in her chest (which, doubtless, caused the dream) and she firmly believed it to be the result of some malignant influence over her by the woman of whom she dreamed.

A white youth, with two or three natives, was drowned in the Chilkat river. A native dreamed that he appeared to him and appealed for food. The dreamer and his friends believed that the drowned were hungry and in need of food, and they cooked a great quantity of beans and bacon, ate some themselves, but cast the most of it into the river to feed the drowned.

In earlier days, ordeals by poison were resorted to in order to determine guilt. Medicines were relied on more for their supernatural than for their medicinal properties; for their charms than for their curative powers. Thus a certain medicine was blown upon traps to make them successful in catching game. Others were used to reveal secrets, to make one rich, to make one successful against his enemy, to give one power to kill animals, to make one happy, and so on almost ad infinitum. Love-potions were concocted and believed to be very efficacious. The writer has been told that many a woman who had a violent hatred for a man has been won to a passionate love for him because he carried a love-potion to influence her.

When fishing, natives talk to their halibut lines, hooks and floats, calling them " brother-in-law," " father-in-law," etc. It is believed that if they did not do so they would not have any good luck.

What has now been submitted does not exhaust the list of Thlinget superstitions. It will serve, however, to show what a sway this evil principle has over the native life. But it is only just to say that many natives no longer take stock in these superstitions.

XVII

TOTEMISM

THERE is no more inter sting and intricate subject pertaining to the natives of Alaska than totemism, and none about which most people have such vague, indefinite and unsatisfactory notions.

The reticence of the natives, their reluctance to talk to white people on the subject and the absence of any written language, make it very difficult to acquire a true and comprehensive knowledge of it. The average white man can find out nothing satisfactory about it by approaching them on the subject. The old natives who know will not respond, and the young ones claim to know nothing about it.

The only way to get at the truth of the matter is to live with them and, indirectly, to draw them out, or let them voluntarily express themselves concerning it. If a white man shows much eagerness to learn about their customs they will almost invariably, especially if they are not well acquainted with him, refuse to talk about them, or tell him some nonsense both to mislead him and that they may smile at his credulity.

Because totem poles consist of carved images, some declare them to be idols. They were never regarded as such, so far as we have been able to learn, by the natives.

An idol is an image of some imaginary deity,

ate
ska
ost
is-

ce
ab-
if-
wl
ut
em
ill
ow

er
m
es
st
or
d

s,
er
o

r,

CHILKAT BLANKET AND WOMAN

and is worshipped as having both being and power. The totem poles of the natives of Alaska, while bearing images of creatures, were never erected to represent any imaginary deity or god. Nor were they ever worshipped. They are highly revered because they carry the tribal emblem. What the coat-of-arms, or crest, is to families of the English aristocracy, so are totemic marks to native families. The Englishman reveres the family crest, but does not worship it; so does the native with his totemic emblem.

Some natives have misled white people by calling their totems idols when they merely meant they were images. The native word for totem is *kō-tē'ä*, meaning image, or likeness. When the natives learned about the idols of the Bible, they used this same word for idol. So now it is used interchangeably for image or idol. As the native does not make the nice discrimination between the meaning of terms that we do, he very innocently says one thing when he means another.

Some have been told by the natives that their people worshipped the totem poles when it was only meant that they have a superstitious reverence for them.

Another thing that would give colour to the belief that they are worshipped is that when they saw the totem of a shaman, they would make a formal sign in its presence, the same as a member of the Russian church makes when he comes into the presence of an edifice or a priest of that faith. The man does not worship the edifice nor the priest; nor does the native worship the pole by so doing.

The nearest approach to idolatry of these people was in attributing to birds, fish and animals supernatural powers, and then setting up images of them. While these creatures are not regarded exactly as gods, yet attributes were ascribed to them equal to the attributes of deity.

" The totem poles," says Professor Dall, in his admirable work, " Alaska and Its Resources," " are in no sense idols. They are like pictures to illustrate the legend that is connected with the family." This view is correct. But they are not only like pictures to illustrate legends; they stand for very much more.

It is very important to a correct understanding of totemism to know the true totemic divisions of the people.

All natives of either main totemic division are regarded as brothers and sisters though they may be of different sub-totems of the division. These cannot intermarry. They must seek partners somewhere in the opposite division, or fraternity.

One of the common errors of writers on the natives is to confound subdivisions with main ones. Another is to use the terms " tribe " and " clan " interchangeably. A tribe may be divided into clans, but not a clan into tribes. A tribe may be composed of several sub-totems but of the same great phratry; a clan, on the other hand, is composed of people of the same totem. Every native has his sub-totem which, in turn, determines the main division to which he belongs.

The entire native population of southeastern Alaska is divided, as already stated, into two great divisions known as the Eagle and the Crow. The sub-totems of the Eagle are the Bear, Wolf, Whale, Shark, etc., and of the Crow, the Beaver, Frog, Salmon, Seal, etc. Every family must both be of the Eagle and the Crow fraternity, the husband of one side and the wife of the other, or vice versa. If the husband's phratry is the Eagle, his wife's must be that of the Crow. Any one of the Crow line of sub-totems may cross over to the line of sub-totems of the Eagle division and seek a wife, and vice versa. But no one of the Crow line can take a partner in marriage from any of the totems of that division or phratry, even though they are utter strangers and no blood relation. That is, one of the Bear totem may not marry one of the Whale, as these belong to the same grand division.

A valuable pamphlet by Mr. J. E. Frobese, at one time curator of the Sheldon Jackson Museum at Sitka, Alaska, gives the following interesting table of marriageable possibilities:

Man's Totem	Woman's Totem
Eagle	Crow
Bear	Beaver
Wolf	Frog
Whale	Salmon
Shark	Seal

A subject so deep and intricate merits and requires something more than a mere glimpse of totem poles from the deck of a steamer to qualify one to pass on it. Totemism is something more than a mere idle and meaningless whim of an ignorant people. With the natives of Alaska, it is the foundation of their entire social structure and a tangible expression of their belief. Its importance among them can scarcely be exaggerated. It expresses their belief in the kinship of men and animals, and had, doubtless, its origin in the belief of the animal ancestry of man. Those of the Eagle division claim to have sprung from the eagle, those of the Crow from the crow. Because of their belief that animals can understand human speech, I have been cautioned more than once, while in camp with natives, and in all seriousness, never to speak in terms of disrespect of the bear, or other animal.

The natives are Darwinians to the very letter. Their belief in the origin of man from animals is expressed not only in their verbal legends, but on some of their totem poles. On one this legend is inscribed:

"Years ago a number of women were in the woods picking berries when a chief's daughter, who happened to be among them, ridiculed the whole bear species. For this affront, a number of bears suddenly appeared and killed all of the women except the chief's daughter. The leading bear of the bunch made her his wife. She bore him a child, half human and half bear. One day this child was discovered up a tree. She was mistaken for a bear, but managed to make her discoverers understand that she was human. She was taken to their village and she became the ancestor of all natives belonging to the Bear totem."

Mr. William Duncan, the "Apostle of Alaska," who speaks with authority on anything pertaining to the natives of Alaska, thinks that totems were adopted to distinguish clans.

"It is not improbable," writes Professor Dall, "that the custom, or system, of totems originated in a desire to prevent war, and to knit the tribes more closely together."

After years of study of the subject and close observation of the working of the system, we are of the firm opinion that totemism had its origin

in the belief of an animal ancestry, and that the
distinguishing of clans, the effort to prevent war,
and the knitting of tribes more closely together
followed as a consequence from its adoption,
rather than suggesting it.

Totemism not only controls marriages, but indicates the rank and caste of people. The higher
the totem pole the greater the man who owns it.
The people of the Hootz (brown bear) family, or
Keet (grampus) family are considered superior
to those of the Hot (salmon) or Chich'g (frog)
family. In public assemblies places of honour are
distributed according to rank (totem). In daily
intercourse, people are treated and respected according to their family totem. Those of an inferior totem are very careful how they speak to
those of a superior one. In the settlement of injuries, totemism plays a very important part.
The man of a superior totem is always awarded
higher damages than one of an inferior crest. In
a drunken orgy a woman had her eye gouged out.
About the same time, another woman, in a drunken
quarrel, had her finger so injured as to necessitate
its amputation. The one who lost her eye, because low-caste, or of inferior totem, was given
only two hundred dollars damages, while the
other, being a high-caste or of superior totem,
was adjudged wronged to the extent of nine hundred dollars.

Totemism governs the amount to be spent on the
dead, what one shall receive at a feast, the paraphernalia he shall wear at a dance, the voice he
shall have in public affairs, the size of his house,
the esteem in which he is held, the naming of
children and native hospitality.

It serves as a fraternal means to bind them

together on the one hand, and to separate them
on the other, and to mark friends from foes. All
of the same great totemic division are friends
and the home of one is practically the home of the
other. No matter where they go, those of their
totem kindly receive them and show them the
warmest hospitality. Those of an opposite totem,
while they may not be regarded as enemies, yet
are not looked upon as friends, nor called upon
for any favour.

A woman of a superior totem, or caste, though
she may live a life of shame and deepest degradation, is respected, and were she to die, would be
deeply mourned and have a costly burial; her
sister of an inferior totem, though she had lived
an immaculate life, would receive scant recognition, and were she to die, would have few to mourn
her death and a shabby burial.

Totemism regulates the disposition of the dead.
Those of the same totem as the deceased must not
raise their hand to do a thing about the body.
Dressing the corpse, making the coffin, carrying
the remains to the grave, digging the grave and
covering it up, or any other thing required, must
be done by those of the opposite totem from the
dead.

Guests must be those of an opposite totem from
the one giving the feast, and they are seated according to caste, or totem.

Totemism proclaims to the world who are the
occupants of a house, and denotes lineage, the
children taking their mother's totem. It regulates what disposition to make of the property
of the dead. It promotes hospitality and sociability, and is a spur to ambition and thrift. Many
a man has laboured and saved in order to erect

a costly totem pole, or to give a big feast, or to throw some glory on his family crest.

Totemism binds them together for mutual help and protection. Every member of a man's totem is ready to contribute of his means and strength to help his friend in time of need. The combined crests of either grand totemic division stand ready, if necessary, to meet the liabilities of any one belonging to their side of the great Thlinget family.

Totemism is recorded history, genealogy, legend, memorial, commemoration and art.

The totem pole is but one of the many expressions of totemism. Everything the native possesses, in many instances even his person, carries totemic designs. He does not make a common halibut hook, or a paddle, a spoon, a bracelet, or scarcely any other object, without etching his totem on it. Why? Because everything he uses is associated with his patron friend and protector, be it eagle, crow, bear or wolf. If he puts the image of his patron on his halibut hook, it will help him to have good success; on his paddle, to go safely over the deep; on his spoon, to protect him from poisonous foods; on his house, to bless his family.

These family crests are represented not only on poles, but on the fronts of houses, on the interior walls, on the prows of canoes and practically all articles used by the natives.

All handiwork in wood, stone, bone, horn, copper, gold and silver bears totemic designs. So with moccasins, baskets and blankets. In this age even marble tombstones are ordered to bear the same. In the burial grounds of natives may now be seen marble monuments (white man totem) with the salmon, the grampus and other totemic figures chiselled on them. Not a few natives have tattooed on their person their totemic patron.

There is no object in the Northland of greater attraction to the tourist, and none which awakens so much speculation, as the totem pole. When a steamer lands at a native village, about the first thing the tourists ask to see are the totem poles. Of these there are four classes—the genealogical, historical (or commemorative), legendary and memorial (or mortuary).

The genealogical pole is usually erected directly in front of its owner's house and, as the name indicates, gives the genealogy of the family within. The wife's totem crowns the top, next the husband's and so on down. Any native walking along and seeing the pole can tell at a glance the clan of the mother, which is the ruling one of the house. From this he will know whether or not he would be welcome to enter and stay there. If the ruling family of the house is not of his totem he passes on. As he reads on down the pole, he learns the totemic connections of the entire household.

The historic or commemorative pole, as the term implies, recounts some special and important event (as regarded by the owner of the pole) in the history of the particular family or the chieftain of the house. Usually such events as thrilling conflicts with man and beast and courageous triumphs are chronicled on these monuments for the consideration of future generations.

The legendary pole, as the term indicates, relates some happy legend particularly prized by the clan of the one who has erected it. Not only are there legends, but songs, that are peculiar to each clan, and the members or votaries of one clan are not allowed to use the legends and songs of the others.

The memorial or mortuary pole, as may be inferred from the term, is a monument erected in the burial-ground to the memory of the dead. It usually carries the single image of the patron animal of the deceased. When cremation was the universal custom of disposing of the dead, cavities were made in the back of the mortuary tablets in which to deposit the ashes of the deceased.

As soon as burial became the general custom the totem pole began to decline, and to-day there are practically no totem pole builders and no new ones are erected.

Totem poles vary in height from a few feet to fifty or more. They are usually very costly, not because of their intrinsic, but for their sentimental, value. In some instances they are valued at three or four thousand dollars each. They are carved out of a solid tree trunk (usually yellow cedar), and by tools of the native's own make, a rude adz being the principal one used. While some are crude in workmanship and hideous in appearance, others are beautifully artistic and pleasing to look upon, showing the workman to be of no mean ability as a carver. Some native villages abound in totem poles, while others have but few, and some none.

The march of civilization is fast supplanting this as well as many other old-time customs of the natives. The totems now standing are in process of rapid decay, being not only covered with moss, but having spruce trees growing out of some, thus marking their age.

At Klinquan are great slab foundations of ancient mammoth communal houses. On the portions of these slabs visible to the eye may be seen wonderful totemic carvings, showing that in olden times even the very foundations of their houses carried the crest of clan or family, wrought there at great pains and expense. Any museum could get valuable relics from this field.

A number of houses are yet seen with the totem of the owner painted or carved on the front gable. The house with a crest thus represented on it is called after the totem it bears. If of the crow it is " *Yalkth-hit* " (Crow-house); of the bear, it is " *Hootz-hit* " (Brown bear-house); of the orca, or grampus, " *Keet-hit* " (Whale-killer-house), and so on.

The brown bear and the grampus are considered the highest symbols of power; the crow, the highest symbol of wisdom, and the eagle, of penetrating vision. All of these are emblems of high-caste families.

The mouse (*kootzeen*) and the snail (*talk*) are symbols of weakness and degradation, and are the emblems of low-caste families.

Slaves were not allowed to erect totem poles, nor was one of a lower caste allowed to erect a pole as high or as elaborate as that of a higher class man. This would be considered a great shame to the higher caste brother, an insult he and his clan would not permit. Instances have been known where ambitious fellows of a lower caste, having erected poles higher than one of a higher caste, have been compelled to take their totems down and shorten them.

When a totem is crowned with a hat, the number of rings on top of the hat indicate the number of important feasts the owner has given.

por-
seen
olden
ouses
there
could

otem
able.
it is
crow
ir, it
orca,
ise),

isid-
the
ene-
igh-

are
the

les,
t a
her
eat
he
ave
ver
of
eir

im-
per

NUMEROUS CURIOS

No clan, or member of a clan, can adopt the totem of another clan with impunity. Wars have been precipitated by such attempts. Less than a decade ago, one clan in Sitka raised the Frog totem which was claimed by another phratry than the one to which the clan appropriating it belonged. Great trouble ensued and bloodshed was averted only by the interposition of the Federal authorities.

A few years ago an audacious native of the Auk village at Juneau had the grampus elaborately painted on the inside of the back wall of his house. This little piece of art originally cost him six hundred dollars; but before he was through with it cost him much more. A terrible commotion followed, as he was not entitled to use the *keet* as his crest. The row was on for a long time, and the affair was finally settled by a money payment.

Some of the reasons assigned for the original adoption of crests are interesting, to say the least. The Kok-won-tons claim that at one time the eagle rendered valuable assistance to a member of that phratry, who in time turned into an eagle. Hence their adoption of this crest.

The Te-qoe-dy claim the grizzly-bear for the reason that a member of their clan married a female grizzly. The Kok-won-tons also claim this as one of their crests, affirming that they acquired the right to it through one by the name of Kät'thlä.

The grampus is the important crest of the Duckla-wady tribe, a branch of the Eagle phratry. They adopted this for the reason that one of their tribe made the first grampus that ever existed, out of a piece of yellow cedar. The Kok-won-tons are

privileged to use this crest also. The great leader
and speaker of the Kok-won-tons at Sitka turned
his *keet ŏnyä'dē tzŏw* (grampus high-caste hat)
into the Sheldon Jackson Museum at Sitka, where
it is one of the interesting objects now seen in
that institution.

A man and his wife of the Kik-sud-dy tribe
were out hunting one day when they heard a song.
They looked for some time before they could locate it. Finally they discovered that it came
from a little frog in the stern of their canoe. The
little songster was taken by the woman and cared
for, and for this reason the frog is the emblem
of the Kik-sud-dies.

The woodworm is the particular crest of the
Gä-nŭk-kä'dies since a woman of their tribe
suckled the legendary woodworm.

Whether the Hydahs originated the crest system and totemism, or borrowed them, we have no
means of knowing. But there are good reasons
for believing that the Thlingets borrowed them
from the Hydahs. Those living near them and
having the most to do with the Hydahs, have the
most totem poles, whereas the farther away you
find them from the Hydahs the fewer they have
and the meaner they are. Then, too, the Thlingets
are not such skilled totemic workmen as the
Hydahs, but are mere imitators.

XVIII

LEGENDS

THE myths and legends of the Thlingets are legion. As they have no written language, all of their legendary lore is handed down to posterity orally and in totemic characters. From time immemorial the people have been fond of relating their folk-lore, so that most of their legends are kept fresh in the minds of all.[*]

Mothers and grandmothers are much given to relating legends to the children. Many of them are told to point a moral and to influence children to obey. Samuel Davis, a native, writes: " One old man begins: ' Once a little boy was all the time playing; when his parents told him to do anything he would not obey; he would have his own way. One day the boy came home about dark. His grandfather told him this world was as sharp as a knife; a little boy might slip upon

[*] " Winter is the time for the gathering of our people at their villages, after being away for supplies of food and other things for their comfort. It is the time given for feasting and paying for work done for the dead. Almost every night there is something going on—either dances, giving of feasts, or some chief gives a smoking party (smoking pipes). Then it is that the old people get in their stories to the children, all sitting around the evening fire after supper."—Samuel Davis.

" At the funeral of Chiefs the traditions and history of the tribe are rehearsed."—" Alaska," by Sheldon Jackson, page 96.

"These people have an oral mythology of the most fabulous character, handed down from father to son."—"Alaska," by M. W. Bruce, page 97.

it any time if not careful. With that the boy began to stamp his foot on the ground, saying, "Grandpa, see how I stamp this ground. There is plenty of room; I can't fall off." While saying these words, something sharp went into his foot, and it became swollen and painful. The next day the boy died, because he would not listen to his grandfather.'

"Then an old woman has her say: 'One time a little boy went trapping with his grandfather (it was a time when people made slaves). They had camped at a certain cove in the evening. The old man thought he could hear some one in the woods behind them, but would not let the boy know, because the boy would be frightened. So the old man said to the boy, "Go down and see if the canoe is well fastened." The old man tried to get the boy down to the canoe first, so he could run after him, throw him into the canoe and push off shore before the people could catch them and make slaves of them; but the boy refused to obey. Again he was told to go down to the canoe, but again he said, "No." The old man, after trying three times to persuade the boy to go to the canoe went himself, jumped into the canoe, and pushed off shore. The people came from the bushes upon the boy and made a slave of him. That is the reason why boys nowadays do as they are told.'"

Again, they are told to rebuke a person for boasting or playing the hypocrite. When one says that he is very old, implying thereby that he knows much, he will be rebuked with the story of the sculpin, which runs thus: *Yalkth* (Crow) saw sculpin on the beach and hid from him to see what he would do. Sculpin swam out on the ocean and went down out of sight. *Yalkth* opened the door of the ocean and went to the house of sculpin, which was under a rock, and said to it, " My younger brother, this is you, is it? " Sculpin disowned him as such. *Yalkth* insisted that he was his older brother. The sculpin said, " I cannot be your younger brother for I am a very old person." The Crow answered: " I want you to be next to me. There will be many sculpins, but you shall be the head one." So the mighty Crow threw sculpin up into the sky, where he is now seen (the Pleiades or the Dipper).

So to one who boasts that he knows because he is old, it is said, " If sculpin could not make Crow believe that he was so old, neither can you make us believe that you are so old and know so much."

Natives say of a hypocritical mourner at a funeral, " He is acting as Crow did when he killed his friend, the deer." The story goes that *Yalkth* saw a nice fat deer, and said to it, " My friend, this is you, is it? " He then invited the deer to cross a deep canyon on a rotten log. The deer objected because he saw that the log was rotten. *Yalkth* walked across it to convince his friend that it would bear him. The deer then attempted to cross, but the log broke and he fell to the bottom of the canyon and was killed. *Yalkth* then went down and feasted on him. After gorging himself, he pretended to be very sorry for the deer and claimed that the wild animals had devoured him.

Stories are told to rebuke and discourage one who shows an ambition to marry another of a higher caste; to inculcate honesty, thrift and self-respect; to warn husbands to be good to their wives lest they should lose them; to keep girls from acting foolishly, etc.

Many of their legends assume to explain the

origin of things and the mysteries of existing phenomena. One tells of the creation of the world. *Yalkth* (the immense imaginary bird) is the mighty Creator.

Other legends claim to give us the origin of man, of the sun, moon and stars, of the whalekiller and of other animals.

For example, the origin of the iniquitous little mosquito is thus given: There was in ancient times a great giant, cruel and very bloodthirsty. His passion was to kill men, drink their blood and eat their hearts.

Many men tried to kill the giant, but were unable to do so until this plan was conceived: A man pretended to be dead and lay down on his blanket. The giant came along and saw him. He felt of the man's flesh and found that he was still warm. Then he began to gloat over him and say, "I will eat his heart and drink his blood." So he lifted up the man, who allowed his head to hang down just as if he were dead, and carrying him into his house laid him down, and then went on some errand.

Immediately the man jumped up and seized a bow and arrow. Just then the son of the giant came in, and he pointed the arrow at the boy's head and asked him where his father's heart was, and threatened to kill him if he did not tell. The boy answered that his father's heart was in his heel.

Then the giant came in and the man shot the arrow through his heel. Just as the giant was dying, he said: "Though you burn me, I will still eat you."

After the giant was dead the body was cremated. Then the man, in derision, took the ashes and threw them to the winds. But each particle of the ashes became a mosquito.

Nearly every tribe has some legend accounting for the origin of their people.

The origin of the Whale tribe is thus briefly told: Many, many years ago, a young Stickeen boy amused himself by carving a small image of a whale and sailing it about on the water. The sport was quietly indulged in from time to time, until on one eventful day the piece of cedar wood turned into a live whale of unusual size and swam away. The boy was surprised and alarmed, of course, and ran home to tell his parents of what had taken place. His father and mother, grown wise as the years had passed over them, knew at once that their son was destined to become a great man; he was to be the father of a new tribe that should spread abroad throughout the land, great and powerful. And so we find it to-day. Branches of the Whale tribe are to be found in many villages, and wherever found they are able to hold their own in the affairs of life.

The totem of the Dā-sĕ-ton' of Killisnoo is the beaver. Some of the tribe captured a small beaver and kept it as a pet. In time it began to compose songs. One day the masters of the beaver found two beautifully carved salmon-spear handles near the foot of a tree by a salmon stream. These were carried home, and when the beaver saw them he claimed that he made them. Something was said that offended him, when he began to sing songs like a person. While he was doing this he seized a spear and thrust it through his master's chest, killing him instantly. Then he threw his tail down upon the ground and the earth on which that house stood caved in. The beaver had dug the earth out from under it. It is from this incident that the Da-se-ton claim the beaver as their crest.

The wolf is the crest of the Kŏk-wŏn-tŏn' tribe. There are two versions of how the wolf came to be adopted as their totem. One is that a member of the tribe met a wolf with a bone in his mouth. "What makes you so lucky?" asked the man. The wolf turned and fled. The following night he dreamed that he came to a very fine village, the village of the Wolf people. The wolf he had spoken to the previous day came to him and told him something to make him very lucky, saying, "I am your friend." He was very thankful for the kind treatment of the man. For this reason the Kok-won-tons have used the wolf for their crest.

The other version is that the man met with some monster wolves while out hunting. One spoke up and told the others not to kill him, and for this reason the wolf is now the tribal totem.

The earthquake is thus explained: Underneath the earth stands an old woman in a bent position. On her back rests a pillar and on top of this rests the earth. *Yālkth*, in an evil mood, tries to shove the old woman from her position. She topples but does not fall. When she topples this causes the earth to quake. If ever *Yalkth* succeeds in pushing her down, the world will come to an end. The name of this Thlinget Atlas is *Hä-tă-yĕ´ shä-nŭk´kō* (old-woman-under).

The Thunder Bird, by flapping his wings or even by moving one of his quills, causes the thunder, and the wink of his eye produces the lightning.

The reason why human beings die is explained
in this manner: The young Crow endeavoured to
make man out of rock and out of a leaf at the same
time, but the rock was slow while the leaf was
very quick. Therefore human beings came from
the leaf, and because leaves wither and die, therefore men grow old, wrinkle and die.

The bluejay came thus by his topknot: *Yalkth*
practised a deception on the squirrel and bluejay.
The latter, becoming angry at this, had the bold-
ness to go to *Yalkth* and upbraid him for it.
Yalkth seized him by the feathers of his head and
pulled them up in a bunch.

The story goes that a man and his wife were
living at a certain fort. Disease had destroyed
their relatives, and they thought to give a great
feast in their memory. One day an iceberg floated
near their dwelling. They took it in and treated
it as a guest. Much oil was poured into the fire,
and dishes of berries and other food were placed
before it. The ice gave forth a squeak that could
not be understood, but was really an invitation
to the dead relatives to partake of the feast. For
this reason when an iceberg drifts near a canoe
the occupants give it tobacco, saying, " *Ok-yeet-
see-e* " (My son's daughter) or " *Ok-yeet-shut'e* "
(My son's wife).

Myths and legends were the first efforts of
primitive man to account for the cause of things.
Crude as some of them are, they yet evince the
awakening of human thought. The myth-builders
were the primitive philosophers. While, in many
instances, their legends are absurd, yet we should
be charitable in our criticism, remembering that
they were originated out of ignorance. They appeared reasonable to the people of their age,

else they would not have been so influenced by
them.

The Thlingets have legends of notable events,
as, for instance, of a flood, from which only a few
people were saved. These became separated,
hence the diversity of speech among them. The
Mount Ararat of this flood is located not far from
Shakan on Prince of Wales Island.

Numerous are their legends of wonderful exploits. Let it suffice to instance only two or three:

Two brothers were hunting when they killed a
porpoise. While skinning it as their canoe moved
along, they saw a devilfish approaching. At once
they prepared to battle with the monster, one of
them handling a spear and the other a sharp knife.
When the devilfish came to the surface and
reached out his tentacles to embrace them, he was
such a horrid-looking creature that the man who
held the knife became frightened and jumped
right into his mouth. He was swallowed up so
quickly that he could do nothing. This left the
brother with the spear to fight the monster single-
handed. He succeeded in killing him, but not until
after the octopus had entwined his slimy arms
around his canoe; so when the dead monster began
to sink he took the canoe with him, too. However,
in due time they all floated up on a narrow point.
Here the devilfish was cut open, when lo, the man
that was swallowed was found alive and none the
worse for his tenancy in the monster's belly.

A certain man caught two whales and tried to
swim ashore with them. After swimming all night
he succeeded in landing them. But when he did
so the raven called and he died. When the raven
croaked his wife knew what had happened, but
she would not go out of the house to see her dead

HOUSE TOTEMS AND INTERESTING OBJECTS

l by

ents,
few
ated,
The
rom

ex-
ree:
ed a
oved
once
e of
nife.
and
was
who
ped
so
the
gle-
ntil
rms
egan
ver,
oint.
man
the

to
ight
did
ven
but
ead

husband. Her mother, however, discovered the two whales and the dead husband, who had now turned into a monster, lying on the beach. Soon all the people heard about the strange creature lying with the whales and went to see it. At last the wife, who was a chief's daughter, went out to the place, crying as she went. The people were astonished at her conduct, and asked: '' What does that high-caste girl mean by calling the monster her husband? '' As soon as the girl came near her mother she said: '' Where are your spirits now? You do not speak the truth. You say that you have spirits when you have none. If you had, this would not have happened to my husband.'' The people became very much excited and listened with great interest to the girl as she talked to her mother. Finally the widowed girl said to the people, '' Some of you that are clean come and help me.'' Her husband had died in the act of holding the jaws of the monster apart. When the people recognized this they were more surprised than ever, and said, '' He must have been captured by that remarkable creature.''

Many of these legends of wonderful exploits are recorded on totem poles. The totem now standing in Pioneer Square in the city of Seattle gives the tale of a devoted girl who lost her life in an attempt to reach the bedside of her dying sister. The latter lived far away on the Nass river. As soon as the sister in health heard of her condition, she set out on the long journey to see the dying one, but her frail canoe was upset on the river and she was drowned. The totem was erected in honour of this brave sister.

Many queer legends are recorded on the totems erected inside of the houses.

On one of these slabs in a house at Kluckwan, a man is depicted in violent action among beasts. The explanation is that a certain man, impelled by taunts, determined to become very strong. To this end he exercised and exposed himself to the rugged elements. He would get out of bed very early in the morning, break icicles from the eaves of the house, place them under his arms and then stand in the cold water of the river. He would then call for the Cold (believing it to have personality) to come from the north. Finally he became strong enough to break the strong part of a tough tree. Then, in time, he went out to fight with whales. He would catch them by the tails and tear their tails apart. Finally he tore the stomach out of one, inflated it and got inside of it and floated off, no one knew where.

While floating around in this stomach (Jonah-like), he composed songs, which are now used as tribal songs by his tribe. This stomach was found (according to the story of the people), and became the property of his tribe. They kept it many years and finally burned it.

In the same village with this curious house totem may also be seen a large mask, the image of the woman who adopted the worm. She suckled this worm as she would a babe, and raised it. When grown, the worm went under the houses and shook them down (an earthquake, perhaps). This woman composed songs that now belong to the Crow tribe. None other than members of this tribe can use these songs.

The tribe had a mask made to represent this remarkable woman. It is now considered a very valuable heirloom. It is ugly, yet no one would be allowed to make fun of it.

It is rather remarkable that while the natives of Kluckwan have made so much of this woman who adopted the worm, yet according to their traditions she lived in the vicinity of Wrangell.

In front of the Sheldon Jackson School, at Sitka, there is a large rock just at the edge of high-water mark. Many, taking the walk from the town to Indian river, sit on this rock as the half-way resting place. It is known as the " Blarney Stone," and is interwoven with several Indian legends.

Mt. Edgecumbe, an extinct volcano within twenty miles or so of Sitka, is the seat of several legends. It is claimed that the old woman who supports the world on her shoulders went down this volcano to the underworld. It is further said that *Tschäk* (the great Eagle) picked up whales out of the ocean and carried them to the top of this distinguished mountain. In verification of this claim, it is said that great heaps of whale bones may be found there.

It certainly is a very inviting spot for the un-tutored mind to conjure with. To the tourist, this venerable volcano is worth travelling many miles to see. On a clear day, as viewed from Sitka, it is a pearl of beauty adorning the landscape.

On a mountain top back of Kluckwan there is a lake which is a fruitful source of mysteries and myths. There are certain rocks in the Chilkat river which are said to be petrified people. These people belonged to the Crow tribe and were coming from the interior at the time of this fearful calamity. Just why they met with this fate, the writer was not informed. Perhaps unguardedly they made fun of some object, or some foolish boast as to what they could do.

In the valley back of the town of Skagway lives
an old woman with a wonderful blowing capacity.
This is why the winds come tearing down the
valley and keep the ground free from snow.
Madam *Skoog-wa* (Skagway is a corruption of
this word) blows it all away when she pleases.

It is remarkable how generally known the legends of the Thlingets are among the people.
Though their country is large and communities
are widely separated, yet the entire people are
familiar with these legends.

Naturally the traditions will vary some as told
by different ones. In substance, however, there
is remarkable agreement.

lives
pacity.
n the
snow.
on of
es.
e leg-
eople.
nities
e are

s told
there

XIX

NATIVE JURISPRUDENCE

IN the accepted sense of the term, there is no such thing as government with the natives.
They have no courts, jails, police nor statutory laws; in short, nothing corresponding to civilized government. They have no such thing as trials. All grievances, offences and injuries are settled according to tribal demand. The tribe or clan takes up its member's cause, and settlements are made according to the nature of the offence, or injury, and the standing of the injured. The tribe of the injured party determines the amount necessary to settlement.

Wounded feelings, as well as injuries of the body and invasion of property rights, have to be atoned for. Any crime may be paid for on a money basis, but while they usually demand life for life, it is not necessarily the life of the murderer. It is more often the life of another, and an entirely innocent person.

If a high-caste native kills one of a lower caste, it is not the one who did the killing that is taken, but one equal in station to the one killed. The same holds good if one of a lower caste kills one of a higher. If one higher than the one killed is taken, then the killing has to go on until it is considered equal.

If a woman kills a man, not the woman, but

some man of her tribe must be taken, as a woman is not considered the equal of a man.

If a man kills a woman, not the murderer, but some woman of his tribe is taken.

An Indian doctor, while drunk, beat the head of his wife to a pulp with a club. The tribe of the murdered woman demanded the life of the doctor's sister. These substitutions were always bravely assumed, as it was regarded great cowardice for one to refuse the office of substitute.

When this sister was informed that she was wanted, she boldly surrendered herself to be killed. In this case, however, the opposite tribe were afraid her people would kill more of them, so the case was settled by a blanket payment.

This was generally the mode of settlement when a rich or high-caste native killed one much inferior to himself.

If a white man kills a native, the murdered man's friends are not particular as to what white man they kill in turn, so they get one whom they deem of equal station. Some years ago, at Wrangell, a drunken row between United States soldiers and natives resulted in the hanging of a native. The friends of the man who was hanged killed an innocent trader. In another case, a white man and his wife were killed by natives because they could not account for the sudden disappearance of two of their number. Because of this custom, more than one white man has mysteriously disappeared in Alaska.

Accidental injuries, or killing in self-defence, must be atoned for precisely the same as if premeditated. A youth accidentally shot and killed his father. His father's tribe immediately demanded the life of the youth (father and son are

roman

r, but

head
be of
doc-
lways
cow-
te.
was
to be
tribe
them,
t.
when
h in-

lered
white
they
ran-
diers
tive.
d an
man
they
ance
tom,
dis-

nce,
pre-
lled
de-
are

JUNEAU, ALASKA

(? opposite tribe). The son was willing to surrender his life, but in this case compassion was shown and the matter settled on a money basis.

Near Angoon, some years ago, a howitzer of a whaling crew burst and killed one or two natives that were employed on the vessel. The natives in turn killed two white men for the accident.

A drunken native, infatuated with a girl, made a fiendish attempt to ravish her. While battering in her door to carry out his brutal purpose, he was shot and killed by her people. For this justifiable piece of homicide, a man had to pay his life, and that man was none other than the girl's husband and natural protector.

If a man commits suicide, a cause is always sought, and he who is regarded responsible for the cause is blamed and his tribe made to pay damages.

In fact no injury or loss happens to a Thlinget, whether intentional or accidental, without his seeking redress and damages. For this reason every Thlinget is liable to blame and damages when, perhaps, he least expects it. Often when they are doing a good turn for one another and are deserving of thanks, their kindness is rewarded with blame. On this account they are very cautious what they do for one another.

A woman on her way from church fell on the ice and hurt herself. For this she blamed the missionary in charge. He had announced the Sunday before that the sacrament of the Lord's Supper would be administered. For this reason she came, and she argued that had she not come she would not have fallen; hence he was to blame.

A girl was invited to go to Haines for her own good. While there she met with an injury with which her friends had nothing to do, by being thrown out of a wagon. The relative that invited her to come to Haines was blamed for the injury and his tribe made to pay damages.

This same girl invited a young man to accompany her from one place to another, the distance being only a few miles. They had to ford a river. While doing so the wagon was swept away, and the young man, and four others in the party, were drowned. The girl was saved. While she was in no way to blame for the accident, yet she was held responsible for the drowning of the young man, and her tribe was called upon for heavy damages.

This feature of their sense of justice strikes one as being not only unjust, but often extremely ludicrous.

A man attended the funeral of another. He felt so sad that he resorted to the whiskey bottle to drown his sorrow. He succeeded in more thoroughly doing so than he had planned; as it killed him. Whether it had more than the usual amount of poison in it, or he drank too much, we do not know. At any rate, his tribe wanted damages for the death of their member, so they held responsible the clan of the man whose funeral he had attended. The argument was that if their man had not attended the funeral he would not have been so sad; and had he not been so sad, he would not have drunk the whiskey; and had he not drunk the whiskey he would not have died. Consequently the family that gave the funeral were to blame.

One native loaned another his gun. The borrower, unfortunately, shot off his finger. The man who loaned the gun was held responsible, as the tribe of the injured man argued that had he not loaned the gun their man would not have lost his finger.

A few years ago one of the small boys of the mission armed with a sling of David's variety was throwing stones toward the ocean, and like the man who shot his arrow in the air, this boy did not know that one of his rocks struck a cordwood splitter on the beach in the head. When it hit the man he tried to die and when he found he couldn't, he went to the mission superintendent and demanded five blankets. The superintendent offered to pay the doctor's bill but refused to listen to any talk of damages. The man departed in a wrathful mood. After several days a relative of the boy who threw the stone called at the office and asked to take the boy from the school. When refused he became angry, declared that he had paid the boy's debts, and now the boy had to work for him. The superintendent, by questioning the man, found that the cordwood splitter had gone to this man and demanded the five blankets and received them. Up to the present date the man hasn't been able to get either boy or blankets from the mission.

A woman hired a young man to convey some lumber on his boat from a certain sawmill to a spot where she wanted to erect a cabin. While he was loading the lumber on his boat, the woman went down on the wharf to look after the matter. On her way a gust of wind caught her and carried her off the wharf and she sustained some injuries. The blame was attached to the young man. The argument was that had he not consented to take the lumber she would not have gone on the wharf; hence his tribe must pay damages.

A native was working in the great Treadwell

mine at Douglas. He quit, and was on his way
to the steamer returning home when he stepped
into the post-office and found a letter containing
a dun for one hundred dollars. Not having the
money, he concluded to go back to work, earn the
money and pay the bill. In less than a week he
fell, with several others, down a shaft in a hoisting
cage and received injuries which paralyzed him
for life. At this writing he is living, but absolutely helpless, and cannot live long. The one
who wrote him the letter is held responsible for
his injuries and will be for his death. The tribe
of the writer of the letter will have to pay heavy
damages.

The son of a chief was shot through the cheek,
merely sustaining a flesh wound; two men, taken
from the tribe of the one who did the shooting,
were killed for the injury. A cut or wound in
the face is considered a matter of the deepest
shame, and heavy liabilities are always demanded
for it.

A high-caste man had the tip of his ear bitten
off in a drunken brawl. A low-caste man was
killed for this injury.

A high-caste woman was accidentally struck by
a man who was lifting an *oolikan* scoop. So keen
was the sense of shame of her people that one of
their clan killed the innocent offender. But in
this instance, the matter did not rest there. The
man's clan made war on the woman's, and several
fell before the mêlée came to an end.

If a father injures his own child, whether accidentally or not, his tribe is liable for damages
to his wife's people. If a husband injures his
wife, his tribe must pay damages to her tribe.

In the days of slavery, any native saved from

drowning, freezing, starvation, or any other form
of death, became the slave of the one who rescued
him.

When a man dies, leaving children, their maternal uncles and aunts assume their support and
care. Another relief from this species of dis-
tress is that the surviving husband or wife takes
another partner without delay.

Some now repudiate this old system, and insist
on holding the property in the family after the
death of either parent. The author has been
called upon more than once to protect both
widowers and widows in their property rights
after the decease of their wives or husbands.

When a Thlinget loans another money, he expects twice as much in settlement, whether the
borrower pays the sum back within a week or ten
years.

A native gives for the purpose of having others
give much more back to him, not so much for
sweet charity's sake, or from any promptings of
generosity. It is considered a shame to those who
receive anything if they do not give back from
four to ten fold more.

A woman gave another an old straw hat. The
recipient did not want the old thing, but dare not
refuse its acceptance for fear of giving offence.
Ashamed to wear it, she put it away in her trunk.
Some months went by, when the donor came and
asked: '' When are you going to pay me for that
hat?''

A young man invited five of his friends to dine
at a restaurant. The meal of each cost twenty-
five cents. After dinner, his guests took him to
a store and each gave him two dollars with which
he could buy anything he wished. They did this

to keep from being put to shame. Large sums are exacted for services rendered about the dead. The most trifling service, such as putting gloves on the hands of the dead, or socks on his feet, or mourning, must be well paid for. Four young men acted as pallbearers for a little child. The mother gave them ten dollars each for this slight service. To build a coffin, dig a grave, erect a grave fence or tombstone commands a large compensation. This is largely due to the fact that the natives are not satisfied unless they spend large amounts on the dead.

If one child injures another, even in play or accidentally, the parents of the injured one demand damages of the parents of the child that committed the offence. Native children seldom quarrel or injure one another when playing, and this law of the people may, in a measure at least, account for it.

Old grievances that supposedly were settled years past are revived for the purpose of extorting money from one another.

Forty years ago a fight took place at a village known as Hootz-na-oo, between two warring tribes. A woman belonging to a powerful tribe of the Sitkans was killed. The life of another, or a heavy payment in blankets, was demanded. The matter was compromised by giving a powerful slave to one of the chiefs of the haughty tribe of the woman that was killed. As the chief prized this slave very much, on account of his strength, this was considered a satisfactory settlement.

The slave served the chief faithfully for years. In the summer of 1908 he suddenly died. The tribe then decided that they had nothing to show for the death of the woman they had lost years

ns are
dead.
gloves
et, or
young
The
slight
grave
ensa-
e na-
large

y or
e de-
that
ldom
and
east,

ttled
tort-

llage
ring
e of
, or
The
rful
ribe
ized
gth,

ars.
The
how
ears

JUNEAU NATIVE BAND

ago and finally proceeded to the village of Hootz-na-oo for another payment. Arriving there, they demanded one hundred blankets. After some powwowing they were paid one hundred and twenty blankets, two Chinese trunks and two guns. They returned to Sitka thoroughly satisfied with what they received. The tribes are now good friends again and peace reigns between them.

In the same village, about fifty years ago, a woman was insulted by a man. She told her people and they counselled her to insult him in revenge. This she did publicly. This precipitated a fight between his people and hers, which resulted in several being killed on both sides. A few days ago a party from the man's tribe came all the way to Juneau (more than a hundred miles) to demand money and blankets from the woman's people on the ground that when they had the fight years ago it was not ended equally, hence they were yet debtors to the man's tribe. It is astonishing how Thlingets will accede to such absurd claims.

If a wife leaves her husband, her people must return all that was given them for her dowry, or its equivalent, to the husband or to his people.

The payment of all artistic totemic work, whether in carving, painting, weaving or engraving, is practically regulated by an unwritten law. All such work is done by those of an opposite phratry and commands extraordinary prices. The latter is due to the skill required for such work, the sentimental value placed on the emblem, and the native's pride in display.

The chief has the ruling voice in the adjudication of all affairs involving the tribe. What he

recommends, the tribe contend for. There is no
cessation of hostilities until a satisfactory settlement has been made. This is one reason why
tribes yield and amicably settle any and all disputes; for with them nothing is settled until both
sides are satisfied.

Thus, although the natives have no legislative,
executive or judiciary department, yet they have
laws, enforce them and readily submit to them.

In this age they sometimes get a double dose
of law, both the white man's and their own. They
have been known to be punished in the courts of
the former and, when they returned to their
homes, be compelled to make satisfaction to the
natives also.

When a native is punished in a white man's
court the aggrieved natives get nothing. This is
not satisfactory. They want as redress for all
injuries a money or property consideration, or
they are not satisfied. For this reason the white
man's court is very unsatisfactory to the average
native. Hence the offender is sometimes
" pinched " twice for the same offence. There
is this, however, to be said in favour of the white
man's law, that when punishment is meted out it
is to the offender, while native redress is demanded of the offender's tribe, who may be altogether inculpable.

XX

MUSIC AND AMUSEMENTS

NO people have greater love for music and amusements than the Thlingets. From time immemorial they have had their own songs. It is surprising how easily and quickly they learn to sing our English songs, hymns and anthems, and to read music. Not a few of them can play the organ well, when they have never taken a lesson.

A few years ago the only thing they had that approached a musical instrument, was a rude drum. Now every native village has its brass or string band, many of their homes have organs, and nearly every one a gramophone or phonograph. In the bands are native boys who cannot speak or read English, yet they master the musical notes without the slightest difficulty.

For the most part, these bands are self-taught. Some native who knows a little more about music than the others is chosen as a leader. They then work out their own musical salvation, not with fear and trembling, but with joy and perseverance. They are so fond of it that they do not consider any amount of practice a task, but a pleasure, so they practise almost incessantly until they become proficient.

Most of them have the gift of song, and some of them have exceedingly fine voices. Congregational singing in our native churches is spirited

and good. Their own native songs at their feasts
and dances are in memory of the dead and about
the exploits of the great and of their patron
animal. Mothers have their lullaby songs which
they sing to soothe their babes to sleep.

Their memorial songs used at feasts and potlatches are very sacred and the people believe
they receive strength from them. They are used
only on special occasions. According to tradition
they were composed at the time of the flood (not
the flood of the Bible, but of native tradition)
and relate the sad events of that terrible visita-
tion, such as the finding of bodies and the separation of their clans. Their songs of more recent
composition are not so significant as their older
ones and are composed from various motives.
They relate mostly to exploits and happenings of
one kind and another, some of them having little
or no significance. The raven, one of their great
patron birds, has much to do with inspiring songs.
When a house was " danced together," as many
songs were sung as motions were made, which,
usually, were four to the right and four to the left.
This was done when a feast was given after the
completion of a house.

Some songs were sung by women only. Much
of their so-called singing is a mere weird chant,
which to the white man is very monotonous and
depressing. The pitch scarcely varies from start
to finish. These chants forcibly remind one of
witches, hobgoblins and spirits. It is the peculiar
construction and genius of their songs rather than
the voices of the singers which make them weird
and uncanny.

All kinds of amusements and sports appeal
strongly to these people. They will give their

last dime to see anything amusing or entertaining,
and they welcome anything that comes along. In
the era when low dance-halls flourished in our
communities, they were largely patronized by natives, in spite of their vileness.

It is this fondness for amusement and enter-
tainment, as well as their respect for their customs, that gives dancing and feasting such a hold
on the people. The white man's dance is now
appealing to them, and not a few are already its
devotees. We fear that it will prove a detriment
rather than a blessing to them.

In their socials, all kinds of amusing games are
played to the unbounded delight of all present.
Their laughter is a spontaneous outburst. They
care little for games that require much mental
effort, and they eliminate from their socials and
entertainments everything not of a comic and
laughter-provoking nature. While they have
many original games of their own, yet they have
appropriated a number from the white people.
Outside, in the proper season, they enter with
zest into all kinds of athletic sports. Some villages have strong ball teams. Fourth of July is
the big day of the year for outdoor sports. They
leave their camps wherever they are and come into
town to celebrate. The sports of the day are base-
ball, canoe-racing, running, jumping, vaulting,
throwing the weight, rock-drilling and other
things too numerous to mention. Every native
who can crawl out of bed is out to enjoy the sights.
Not one of the long list of sports does he miss
if he can help it. This is the day when all are
dressed in their best. Dresses and new suits are
bought for the occasion. The celebration over,
they are then carefully put away in a trunk,

not to be worn until the holiday comes round again.

In their socials, the most popular of their own games is what they call " *ha-goo* " (come here!). They choose sides, having from ten to twenty or more on a side. Each side chooses a leader, who is given a flag. This leader stands out in front of those on his side. Then the name of some one on the opposite side is called out with the invitation—" Ha-goo "—to come and take away the flag without smiling if he can possibly do so. When he approaches to take the flag they do and say all sorts of funny things to make him smile. If he smiles, he has to leave his party and join the side with the flag. If, on the other hand, he succeeds in taking the flag without smiling, then all that have been captured from his side are released to go back to the side from which they were taken. In this way they try to pull over the entire opposite side, and the side which succeeds in doing this is the winning one. This game affords them lots of amusement. Some start out with a very serious face, determined to get the flag without smiling, but have to succumb before they succeed as they meet the volley of jokes, witticisms and wry faces. Then comes the laugh for all.

The girls play with their dolls and toys of all kinds, and the boys play ball, marbles, fly kites and indulge in all kinds of childish games. Coasting and skating are favourite winter sports. Roller-skating is quite a fad with the native boys and girls. In several places in the territory there are large rinks run by white men, and they are liberally patronized. But dancing is the most popular amusement of all.

Many of their games are games of contest. This is carried into their dancing. They also have eating contests. The original native spoon is a very large affair, practically a ladle, carved out of wood or horn. One of these will hold a half pint or more of seal oil. At times they vie with one another to see who can drink the most spoonfuls of this nauseating oil.

They are very fond of jokes and witticisms. In their feasts and other public gatherings they have a great deal of speech-making, like the guests at a fashionable banquet. These speeches are characterized by wit and humour that frequently elicit the loudest applause. Of course some of their remarks that would sound tame to us strike them as being very clever.

In this connection it may not be out of place to mention some incidents, amusing and otherwise, that have .e under our notice.

A noted woman of Sitka prayed openly in prayer-meeting that God would forgive her for the sins she had in mind to commit the following week.

A pupil of one of our mission schools reported that another boy had sworn at him. The culprit was summoned before the superintendent and admitted that he was guilty. When asked what evil things he had said, he replied that he called his accuser " ham and eggs." He was dismissed with the injunction to go, and " swear " no more.

At a funeral we saw a woman, as we were leaving the house with the corpse, pick up a phonograph and take it along with her. As we had seen them carry all kinds of things to place in and around the graves of their departed ones, even sewing-machines, we naturally thought she was carrying the phonograph for the same purpose. But as soon as the coffin was placed in the wagon that was to bear it to the cemetery, the music box was placed on top of the coffin, a youth jumped into the wagon from behind, wound up the machine, put on a record and set it to squeaking out a funeral march. When this was played through it was started again, and was kept playing until we arrived at the grave. As soon as the body was committed to the grave, it was set to playing again, and when we left the cemetery the machine was doing its utmost to soothe their sorrowing hearts.

In some towns it has become very stylish to hire a hearse; a luxury which costs ten dollars. Recently we held a funeral at which they started to carry the coffin to the cemetery, a distance of about a mile. The procession had not gone more than a quarter of the way when all at once it was decided that they should have the hearse—not so much to relieve the men who were carrying the coffin, but for the looks of the thing. It was a cold, stormy day, with a foot or more of snow on the ground. The coffin with the corpse was dropped in the snow and the procession kept waiting near it while the hearse was brought to convey the remains the rest of the way to the cemetery. It took nearly an hour to get the vehicle, and all that time the procession stood there in the snow and storm.

We see queer things, not only at burials, but also at weddings. It is rather odd to see two old people who have lived together for thirty or forty years and have, perhaps, four or five children, stand up to be married. Yet this has been done in several instances. They had lived together in the Thlinget way, but they wanted to be married the white man's way.

At one marriage, the bride, seeing that the ceremony was about to be closed, produced a ring to be placed on the bridegroom's finger.

At the same wedding the bridesmaid turned her back to the officiating minister while the rest of the bridal party stood, as they should, facing him.

Some are so clumsy that they blunder in trying to get into position and in trying to clasp hands where the ceremony calls for it.

At a christening, just as the minister was about to apply the water, a boy of four years took fright and ran at the top of his speed down the aisle and out of the church.

In prayer-meetings we have seen mothers praying (standing, with eyes closed) with babies from a year to two years old kicking and squirming in their arms enough to jolt every idea out of the head of the ordinary white woman; yet they have kept right on praying until their entreaty was through.

On one occasion we saw a man who was blocked in a seat by three women get up and climb over the backs of several seats in order to get out; and that in the presence of a large congregation. This he did rather than ask the women to let him pass. To speak to the women would, in his estimation, be a great breach of propriety, but climbing over the seats was nothing out of the way.

Their dogs frequently come to church and sometimes it requires much ingenuity to get them out. Right in the midst of the service some one will collar a dog or grab him by the tail and drag him out of the sanctuary with as much gravity as if it were part of the service.

When the natives saw a steamboat for the first time they took to the woods through fright. They thought it was some huge being that would bring a terrible disease, such as smallpox. For this reason they pulled a certain native vegetable that resembles our carrot and is peppery, and looked through them at the steamboat, believing that this would protect them from the disease. They were amazed when they saw men walking about on the "fire-canoe."

The phonograph was a great wonder to them when it first came, and they flocked to see and hear the wonderful box that could talk and sing. They readily paid a quarter to hear a single tune, and one white man reaped a financial harvest from them for letting them hear his machine.

The first negro that appeared in their country was a great puzzle to them. They held all kinds of theories as to what made him black. Some maintained that he had lived where there was too much smoke; others that he lived in a house whose only entrance was a chimney, and that he became black by going in and out.

When they first saw a man with a wooden leg, they regarded him not only with wonder, but thought him a very comical sight.

The man who could take off his hair (wig) was a greater wonder to them, however, than the man with the wooden leg.

But the most wonderful of all, and the one that afforded them the most amusement and most excited their curiosity, was the man who could take out his teeth. One of them made the discovery that a certain storekeeper could do this. He soon

spread the news among his people, and they
flocked to the store to see the wonderful man.
They even bluntly asked him to take out his teeth.
Seeing his opportunity to attract them to his store
as patrons, he did so. Their amazement knew no
bounds when they saw him take out of his mouth
a full set of uppers, gum and all, and then replace
them. Every native in the country soon heard
of this remarkable man, and many of them made
an excuse to buy something just to get an opportunity of seeing the storekeeper remove and replace his teeth. It proved to be a sple did " ad "
for him.

These incidents will serve to show how impres-
sionable they are. It may be truthfully said that
the native, with his little, gets more real enjoyment out of life than do many of our wealthy
white people with riches at their command. He
has fewer wants and cares, and, above all, is not
greedy for riches. Hence we find more content-
ment and true enjoyment of life in the homes of
these humble people than in many homes of our
own race.

XXI

MORALITY

IT cannot be denied that "latitude and longitude make broad differences as to what constitutes vice and virtue." The ethics of the Chinaman do not altogether correspond with those of the American. The lower the scale of civilization the wider the difference in what constitutes vice or virtue.

So we find the Thlingets of Alaska measuring actions by a different standard from our own. What would shock us they regard as eminently proper. On the other hand, what we approve they would condemn.

They see no impropriety in a man living with a woman some months with the view of marrying her providing she suits him. We see no impropriety in a man escorting another man's wife under certain circumstances, whereas they think this altogether improper and reprehensible.

Thousands of our people of both sexes go in bathing together right in public every summer. Nothing could be more shocking to the natives of Alaska than this.

We think it is altogether proper for brothers and sisters not only to speak to each other, even after the sister becomes a woman, but to show their affection for one another. The Alaskan natives, on the other hand, consider it the proper thing for a brother to sit with his back to his sister or his mother-in-law; if he needs to communicate with them it must be through a third party, or in such a manner as if he were not addressing them.

It is regarded a shameful thing for a married woman to speak to a man other than her husband, or to be seen in the company of another man for even a moment.

Our young girls and ladies may have their beaux and talk with their gentlemen acquaintances as much as they like and no harm is thought of it. The Thlinget girls cannot do this without being branded as immoral.

To marry one of the same great totemic phratry, though no blood relation, is a matter of deep disgrace, and in earlier times one who violated this custom was punished with death. Any who offend in this matter now are deeply execrated.

We recall a case where two cousins of the same phratry married. They loved each other and were married according to the white man's law. But their own people turned bitterly against them for this, and scorned the girl f   the day of her marriage until her death.

A wife is greatly disgraced if she is cast off by her husband, though she may be altogether undeserving of such treatment. For this reason wives often endure very brutal treatment from their husbands.

It is considered a very shameful thing for a woman to expose her person even to her husband or to another woman. Women suffer and die, even in childbirth, rather than submit themselves to a doctor.

Sweeping charges of immorality have been made against the natives of Alaska. This is no more just than to declare the same of white people because some are bad. Even though a majority of them were immoral it would not justify us in saying they were all so. It were as just for them to declare that all the white people are drunkards because they see so many who are. Sweeping statements are seldom true or just.

It is said that the women have no regard for chastity, but their system of ethics is largely to blame for this. It is not considered improper for a man and woman to live together, though not married. Consequently some use this as a license for improper sexual relations. There are, however, those who are chaste and would not barter their virtue for any price. While prostitution is practised, it is not advertised and fostered as it is with civilized races.

It should be remembered that the natives have not been long acquainted with our system of marriage. Their own was without rite or ceremony. In many instances a mere mutual understanding between the parties living together that they were husband and wife was all there was to it. This never offended the public conscience so long as the parties showed good faith.

Nearly every race has a different marriage system from all the others. Uncivilized communities, from the very nature of the case, cannot know of the Christian form until it is introduced. They are obliged to hit upon some system, crude as it may appear to us. The Thlingets adopted the dowry system that prevailed in the time of Jacob. This is just as sacred in their eyes as the Christian system is to us. Under it native men and women have lived together for thirty, forty and fifty years in good faith, and reared large fami-

eople
ority
as in
them
:ards
ping

l for
ly to
r for
not
ense
how-
arter
an is
as it

have
mar-
ony.
ding
were
This
the

sys-
ties,
v of
'hey
is it
the
cob.
ris-
and
and
mi-

lies. They could not have done better had they
been married by a dozen priests. And yet we
meet white people who regard the native system
as a system of fornication.

There are no parents in all the world that guard
their girls more carefully in order to preserve
their chastity than the Thlingets of Alaska. If
they did not value virtue they certainly would not
be so careful to protect it. As soon as a girl approaches womanhood she is kept under constant
surveillance. She is not allowed to go off by herself anywhere. She is under the eye of her
mother, or aunt or sister until she is married. It
seems to us that this shows some regard for
virtue.

It is true that much coarse, vulgar and indecent
sensuality obtains with some, but more from
drunkenness than election. Women are debauched,
but are not willing parties to the transaction.
The appetite for strong drink is the curse and
ruin of many of them, and has betrayed many a
woman to part with her virtue. Men, knowing
their weakness for liquor and how helpless they
are when under its influence, use this means of
taking advantage of them.

The sale and the giving of liquor to the natives
is the most debasing of all influences that they
encounter. There is a stringent law against it,
and public opinion in Alaska is strongly with the
law, yet there are men so low (white men, we are
sorry to say) that they are constantly violating
this law. The courts are doing their best to stamp
out this criminal practice and have succeeded in
sending many of these offenders to the peniten-
tiary. But in spite of their strenuous efforts to
break it up, the traffic in liquor with the natives

continues with most baneful and degrading results.

This curse has hung like a pall over them since the advent of the Russians. Before the coming of the white man they were strangers to liquor in any form. The art of brewing and drinking it was acquired. Ballou, in his volume on Alaska, states that the Russians taught them to make quass. Bancroft, in his history of Alaska, claims that they were taught the art of distilling by United States soldiers.

Whoever is responsible for their knowledge of manufacturing drink, it is certain that they knew nothing of it until they were taught it by members of the superior race.

Another undeniable fact is that they have been encouraged to drink by the example, not only of white civilians, but of soldiers who were sent to Alaska to maintain law and order. Bancroft, in his history of Alaska, has shown that the soldiery have much of the debauchery of the natives to answer for. Governor Swineford, and other writers on Alaska, bear witness to the same unpleasant truth. Scores of citizens have made the same observation. It is certainly regrettable that men who are sent out by our government to enforce law and order should be the very ones to drink and carouse, create drunken brawls, strife and discord in communities where they live. That this has been done times without number in Alaska, no one can deny.

The government makes a ludicrous mistake in thinking the miners of Alaska need the soldiery to restrain them from acts of violence. As a class their behaviour is far superior to that of the soldiery.

There are some fine fellows wearing the uniform, and the officers, with scarcely an exception, are true gentlemen. But too many rowdies are in the ranks, and such should not be employed to conserve law and order. As soon as they are loose from duty, they make for the saloons to drink, carouse and do violence.

It is a question whether Alaska has profited or suffered more from the army. Bancroft and other careful writers think the latter is true.

"There are plenty of irresponsible whites," writes Ballou, "ready to make money out of the aborigines. Rum is the native's bane, its effect upon him being singularly fatal; it maddens him; even slight intoxication means to him delirium and all its consequences, wild brutality and utter demoralization."

More crimes, cruelty, brutality and misery among the natives are due to drink than to any other one thing—yea, than to all other things put together. Many have died directly from over-drink and poisonous drinks. Many have been killed in drunken brawls or crippled for life. Children are abused, neglected and made to suffer by drunken parents.

The teachers and missionaries who live and labour among the natives have many sad cases of brutality and suffering, all through drink, brought to their notice.

Theft is little known among them. Before the fine art of thieving was introduced by the white man, no man's house was ever robbed, nor his wood stolen though cut and banked in the forest; his garden was not plundered, though miles from his home, nor his blankets thrown over his canoe to protect it from the sun disturbed, nor any of his belongings appropriated by another. Valuable articles are deposited in deadhouses and on and around graves, articles that natives covet, yet these were never stolen. The example of white crooks and thieves is pernicious and has encouraged some natives to imitate them. Much thieving has been laid to their door, when in truth it belonged to white rascals.

The percentage of thieving by natives is much lower than that of the white races. For more than twenty years we have lived among them. Our doors have been left unlocked for them to walk in and out; frequently we were out and they had the house all to themselves, yet in all these years we have never had anything stolen by one of them.

While many have been brought into court for drunkenness, disorderly conduct, fighting, assault, etc., yet very few have been tried for theft. The crime of murder has been committed by them, but not so often as by white men in their country. In most cases this crime, when committed by natives, was because they were under the influence of liquor. It is safe to say that as many natives have been killed by white men as white people killed by them.

A man committed suicide simply to make trouble for one who offended him. According to native custom, if a person commits suicide because some one has offended him, or opposed a wish of his, heavy damages or a life must be given to the tribe of the suicide by the tribe of the one giving the offence. So suicide is sometimes resorted to in order to harass and burden others. The threat of suicide is sometimes used as a bluff to get one's way.

There are a few native girls who imitate their

fallen white sisters. They barter their virtue, and some of them, when they find themselves trapped, resort to abortion. This they do, not by applying to a physician, as we have no physicians who would abet a native girl in this, but by personal efforts and by taking native concoctions. They are not always successful, as too many children without visible fathers testify.

The native " tough " is becoming scarcer and scarcer, and has always been frowned on by the great body of natives. The natives no more approve of their girls leading a bad life than the white people do of their girls. While there may be yet a few native girls who lead a fast life, the number is small as compared with those who were once given to it. Some of them have been brought into the church, reformed and transformed, and for years have led a clean life. They have settled down, content to be the wife of one man and rear children.

Among the white people of Alaska, the natives have the reputation of having little regard for the truth. Their testimony in court, unless corroborated by the testimony of a white person, will not be considered by the average juryman. We have found from experience that while it is true the word of many is unreliable, yet there are those who can and do speak the truth, and whose word may be depended on. But we admit, with regret, that many will prevaricate if they think there is anything to be gained by it, or to injure one for whom they have ill will.

One of their most reprehensible faults is their failure to meet their financial obligations to white men. Merchants who have given them credit, and friends who have loaned them money, have found all too late that but few of them have the honour to square their accounts. They seem to think it is legitimate for them to " beat " a white man. Of course there are some who will pay without coercion their just debts. Among themselves they pay, as they cannot get away from it.

Profanity, smoking and chewing tobacco, and drinking are acquired vices. They are not as yet very profane. But they hear profanity so much from white men that it sticks to them to some extent. Some use profane words without knowing that they are reprehensible. This is seen in speaking to the missionary in whose presence they would not use " bad " words if they knew them to be such.

Not a few are addicted to smoking, but very few chew tobacco. The older women are particularly fond of snuff, and some of them use the pipe also.

It is only just to say that among them there are those who eschew all of these evils and live good moral lives.

XXII

DISEASES

WHILE certain diseases have always been found among the Thlingets, others that now afflict them are of recent introduction. Tumours, cancers and toothache were unknown to them until within recent years. The older ones have yet sound and excellent teeth while the rising generation experience the white people's misfortune of cavities, toothache and dental torture.

A certain woman eighty years old or more, and known to us, has never had the toothache, and every tooth in her head to-day is as sound as a dollar. On the other hand, a woman yet in her twenties has had half of her teeth extracted and several of the remaining ones filled. The white man's food, especially his sweetmeats, which are now freely indulged in by the natives, is, no doubt, largely the cause of this change.

While consumption is now the most prevalent disease among them, we are told by the natives themselves and by careful historians that it is an imported disease. "The Indian calls tuberculosis 'the white man's disease,' and so far as I have been able to learn it was practically unknown to him in his uncivilized state." It is common to hear consumption spoken of among our own people as "The Great White Plague." This would

221

indicate that it is surely the white man's disease. Whatever its origin with the natives, it is certain that it has a fearful hold on them.

Dr. Paul C. Hutton, surgeon and physician at Fort William H. Seward, Haines, Alaska, in a published report for the year 1907, states that he found on investigation 20.6 per cent of the natives of that place afflicted with undisputed tuberculosis, 12 per cent of probable cases of pulmonary form, and 16.2 per cent of tuberculosis other than pulmonary.

While every village has its quota of consumption, yet we are very sure no other village can match this. We have been reliably informed that there are more cases of venereal diseases among the natives in that community than in any other. If so, this would account for the prevalence of consumption there.

While this disease, without a doubt, carries off to-day more natives than any other, yet we know that it is not so bad as it was a decade or more ago. The natives clothe themselves better, take greater precautions against getting wet and catching colds, live under better sanitary conditions and employ competent physicians far more than they ever did before. This naturally tends to lessen the prevalence of the disease. Other physicians of eminent ability declare that Dr. Hutton's report is an exaggeration. They found that cases which were considered by him as consumptives were not such at all. The author is positive that the mortality among the natives of southeastern Alaska, at least, is not extraordinary. Some sickness and death must be expected. Of course these should be diminished to the fullest extent. But to raise the cry that the natives are

disease.
certain

cian at
a, in a
that he
natives
abercu-
nonary
er than

nsump-
ge can
ed that
among
other.
nce of

ies off
know
more
, take
catch-
ditions
e than
nds to
Other
. Hut-
d that
con-
hor is
ves of
inary.
l. Of
fullest
es are

dying as if smitten with the plague is neither true nor wise.

If there were the least doubt about consumption being an imported disease, there can be none about smallpox. The scourge was introduced, according to Bancroft,* in the year 1836. Since then it has appeared from time to time with more or less virulence. The last epidemic of smallpox was in the summer of 1901, when scores were carried away by it. The natives travel about so much and are so careless about spreading diseases that when this loathsome disease breaks out it soon goes from one end of the country to the other. Their communal style of living and the unsanitary conditions of their villages highly favour it. For these reasons, when it breaks out fearful mortality results from it.

All forms of venereal diseases are legacies of the white man to the natives. Diseased sailors from Russian ships and American whalers introduced them. Being contagious, and the natives being so indifferent to the spread of diseases, venereal afflictions are common. Much of it now is inherited. Thus the sins of their fathers are visited upon their children.

The prevalence of syphilis is no sign of wholesale immorality, as it spreads by contagion and inheritance, and many innocent ones, as is seen among the children, are tainted with the disease. The careless, uncleanly life of the average native favours its spreading and perpetuation.

Measles and whooping-cough are imported diseases, and very few native children now escape them. Measles is very serious with them, as it frequently terminates in pneumonia or consumption.

* "History of Alaska," page 560.

The original diseases of the Thlingets are pneumonia, rheumatism, scrofula, blood diseases, ophthalmia, neuralgia and pulmonary hemorrhages. Strange to say, fevers such as typhoid, scarlet, malarial, etc., are scarcely known in Alaska. We would naturally suppose that fevers of this nature would thrive among a people so untidy in their homes, but such is not the case. It may be accounted for on the grounds that the temperature never rises high enough to create excessive heat and rank decomposition of dead vegetation; that the prevalent rains purify the atmosphere; that they live on beaches swept by tides, and that they have the purest water in the world for drinking and cooking purposes. Of course we now refer to the natives of the coast.

We frequently see Thlingets afflicted with tuberculosis of the hip. Ophthalmia is a prevalent disease, much of it, we believe, being due to smoke. Comparatively speaking, only recently have the natives employed stoves. Their life was practically spent around an open fire, in the house as well as outside. They could scarcely sit around these fires without being more or less enveloped with clouds of smoke.

Pott's Disease is another form of tuberculosis which we meet with among them. For this reason we see humpbacks everywhere, and not a few have died from tuberculosis in this form.

Seldom do we find cases of insanity and idiocy among the natives. Where insanity has manifested itself disease has been at the bottom of it. They certainly are not driven to it from worry, like so many of their white brothers. Aside from some petty annoyances, they have little to worry about. The simple life, as a rule, gives slight occasion for serious mental disturbance. The inmates of our insane asylums come mostly from our more complex civilization.

The natives have no knowledge of, and, apparently, no concern about, sanitation. "Discarded garments and old shoes lying rotting in the moist soil; salmon skins and salmon flesh disintegrating; tin cans partially filled with stinking slush and half buried; rotten logs and decaying organic matter everywhere. Both inside and out we find everything conducive to the propagation of germs." *

"From a free open life they were changed to a life in huts and houses crowded so closely and with so little ventilation that probably half a dozen or more would have to breathe air which from a hygienic point of view would not contain sufficient oxygen to properly support one life."

The unknown author of this latter quotation is correct. A lack of the appreciation of the value of good, sweet, fresh air is no doubt responsible for not a little sickness among them.

As Dr. Hutton points out, in the quotation above, their carelessness about the removal and disposition of garbage is also a fruitful cause of disease.

"These Alaskans," writes Ballou, "have no idea of sewerage, or of the proper disposal of domestic refuse. All accumulations of this sort are thrown just outside the doors of their dwellings, to the right and left, anywhere, in fact, which is handiest. The stench which surrounds their cabins, under these circumstances, is almost unbearable by civilized people, and must be very unwholesome."

* Hutton.

A campaign has been inaugurated by the government school authorities against this unsanitary condition in native villages. But unless there is some way to enforce obedience to established rules and regulations little will be accomplished, if we may judge by the results from efforts of others along this same line. The natives, while inclined to listen, give very little heed to any hygienic and sanitary instructions.

They have no knowledge of medicine, proper nursing or caring for the sick. In their efforts to help the sick, their remedies, aside from the rites of shamanism, are very crude and simple. They gather herbs and apply them to the sick, sometimes raw and sometimes cooked. They also steep roots and herbs and use the liquor from them for medicine. The old women are their chemists. They mingle not a little superstition in with their concoctions. For scrofula the inner bark of the devilclub and oil were outwardly applied. The bark was dried and ground to powder. Bleeding was, and is yet, a popular practice. The writer knows of one native, a leading man in his community, whose shoulders and back are full of scars, the result of cuttings for the purpose of bleeding. For six or eight years, every fall when he has returned from his summer's fishing, he has called in one of the local physicians (white) to do the cutting, and by request of the native himself I have stood by and witnessed some of these operations. The malady he has each time sought relief from by this drastic method is rheumatism or sciatica. In every instance he has found relief. The man apparently is well and strong to-day. He is probably forty-five or fifty years old.

It is rather strange that when they used to bind
up their cuts and wounds with dirty rags, and
were little protected from filth, there was so small
a percentage of peritonitis among them. Now,
with antiseptics, sterilized instruments and the
best of care, blood poisoning is not infre-
quent.

In treating ulcers and running sores, they insert
a bunch of eagle's down into the heart of the sore
and leave it there until it is well glued to the pus.
Then they draw it out, bringing with it all the
pus that has attached to it. This opens up the
sore in such a manner as to let the bad matter
run freely out.

They make an abundant use of the natural
mineral springs which are found in the country.
For years, if not for generations, they have been
acquainted with the medicinal value of these
springs.

" Twenty miles south of Sitka," wrote Ballou
more than twenty years ago, " on the same island,
there are a number of hot springs, strongly im-
pregnated with iron and sulphur, the sanitary nature of which has been known to the Indians for
centuries, and hither they have been in the habit
of resorting for the cure of certain physical ills,
especially rheumatism, to which they are so
liable." The hot springs near Hoonah and Killisnoo are also well patronized by natives.

The steam bath is very popular with them.
They take a number of springy sticks or poles and
make a frame the shape of a large round-top bee-
hive. Over this they throw a small canoe sail or
piece of drilling, thus making a booth large
enough for two or three to crawl inside. Several
good-sized hot stones are placed inside. Then

they crawl in themselves and steam to their heart's content.

Some practise fasting, when sick, going for days with little or no food. It has a good effect, too. If there were more fasting and less stuffing there would be fewer dyspeptics and less illness.

They have what are called "rubbers." These are usually old women who profess to be able, by rubbing the person with their hands, to effect cures. They claim to be especially effective with any kind of stomach trouble. These rubbers are often employed and they make a good charge for their services.

They have practically no knowledge of nursing the sick. The sick are given to eat whatever they ask for, whether it is good for them or not. They humour them and think it is wrong to deny them anything they call for. If prescribed for by a physician, the medicine is very poorly administered. It is not given regularly nor in quantity according to the prescription. If the patient does not recover after taking one or two doses of medicine, both the medicine and the doctor are considered useless, no matter how chronic the disease may be. Almost invariably the bed of the sick is made on the floor, while the bedstead is used for holding boxes and other chattels. They are often kept in a stifling atmosphere not fit for a well person to breathe, with a dozen or more people tramping about, talking and making more or less noise in the room. They are allowed to get up and go out in the wet and cold, even when so weak from wasting disease they can scarcely stand on their feet. Nothing has been more pathetic than to see natives emaciated from disease tottering about endeavouring to wait on themselves when they should have been in bed and waited on. This is due to four things: lack of conveniences, neglect, false modesty and ignorance.

A well-equipped, up-to-date hospital should have been erected for the Alaskans long ago by the United States government. It is a crying shame that it was not done. The mere sense of humanity should have prompted it, if not a desire to perpetuate the race. If only an infinitesimal part of the millions that have been wasted on gunpowder alone could have been used for such a purpose, it would be far more to the credit of our government.

A small one, capable of caring for about fifteen patients, has recently been established in the capital city, Juneau. To meet the needs of the people other sections should be supplied with hospitals. Alaska is a country of magnificent distances, and natives can hardly be expected to carry their sick three or four hundred miles for treatment. The facilities for travel are such that it takes days and even weeks to go from some points to Juneau. The expense also is not light. One hospital, however, is better than none, and we are grateful for the one that is in operation.

Some physicians claim that the constitution of the native requires twice as much medicine to the dose as that of a white person in order to produce the same effect. We know of a native woman who took half a teaspoonful of laudanum to produce sleep, but without avail. The same woman took strong morphine pellets according to prescription for the same purpose, yet they had no effect on her. So this claim may be true.

In southeastern Alaska the climate has much to do with the health of the natives. The excessive humidity is a fruitful source of rheumatism, colds, coughs and consumption. Travelling almost altogether in open boats, their clothing becomes saturated with water; they chill and a heavy cold results. The women are far less careful in protecting themselves than are the men. While the latter are seen knocking around in slickers and tight rubber boots, the former will be in their bare feet and scantily clad.

Freaks are found among the natives as well as among other people. We frequently see blind natives, but seldom meet with deaf ones. During our long residence in Alaska we have never met with a native mute. They are especially blessed with a good faculty of speech.

Blindness is sometimes inherited, and sometimes brought about by accidents and disease. For the hopelessly blind people and the indigent there should be a home where they might receive proper care and have some of the comforts of life. As it is, they must be a burden to their people and grope around as best they can.

It only remains to be said that there are some natives who live on a higher plane of life than the average. These know better how to care for themselves in sickness, have better homes and more conveniences and employ good physicians. As along other lines, so in the care of themselves and their sick, they are advancing.

XXIII

RELIGION

HE who writes about the natives of Alaska without noting their religion gives a very deficient account of them; religion has been and is yet a great factor in their lives.

Man is by nature a religious being. In every clime and in every race he selects some object, real or imaginary, to propitiate. He either clothes some object of nature, man, beast, sun or fire, with supernatural powers, or evolves beings out of his own imagination whom he thus clothes.

These he propitiates in proportion as he believes they have power to harm. Thus men naturally grope after the Supreme Being, " if haply they may find Him." The Thlingets of Alaska are no exception to the rule.

They had no temples, no religious assemblies, no representations of deity, in short, no rites or ceremonies that might properly be called religious, in early days. They were truly heathen.

They have been called demonologists, or devil-worshippers, but they never worshipped demons nor the devil. They had no idea of the latter until they learned about him through the teachings of the Russian missionaries.

Some have said that their religion was spiritualism. While they firmly believed (and do yet) in spirits, yet it can hardly be said that this belief attained the dignity of a religion. The Thlinget mind clothes everything, inanimate as well as animate, with spirit.

The belief in the existence of evil spirits is the foundation of shamanism. They propitiate and conjure with these imaginary evil spirits in order to purchase their good will, but they do not worship them. Shamanism is one grand effort to wrestle with these supposed evil spirits and obtain immunity from them. But their belief in the existence of spirits was never elevated into a religion.

"Their aboriginal belief," writes Ballou, "is called Shamanism, or the propitiating of evil spirits by acceptable offerings. It is significant that the same faith is participated in by the Siberians, on the other side of Bering Strait. This is no new or original form of religion; it was the faith of the Tartar race before they became the disciples of Buddhism."

It is but a step from spiritualism to a belief in ghosts. The Thlingets believe firmly in the latter. *Goosh-ta-kah* (Land-otter-man) is their chief hobgoblin. The spirits of the drowned linger around in the forests near the watercourses until they finally go way back into the interior.

The Thlingets have been called ancestor worshippers. While they have a profound respect and reverence for their departed ancestors, yet they do not worship them. They believe in the continued existence of their spirits after death, and even call on these spirits for favours, but this belief never led them to worship the departed as our Catholic constituency worship saints.

Again, they have been called animal worshippers. "They seem to entertain," writes Ballou, "a sort of animal worship, a reverence for special birds and beasts." But they do not worship these objects. They may be said to approach it because of their reverent and prorᵢtiatory attitude toward the animals adopted as totems. Their belief in an animal ancestry, as already shown, is doubtless the foundation of this adoption, while the propitiation is due to the adoption and to their regarding the creatures so adopted as clothed with supernatural powers. The ancient Egyptians were real animal worshippers because they had them represented in their temples and made obeisance to them as they would to deity. So far as we have been able to learn, the Thlingets never did this. Strictly speaking, they were not animal worshippers.

Nor were they Nature worshippers, as some have declared them to be. The sun, moon, clouds, tide, etc., are thought of as possessing spirits because they seem to be instinct with life, but they were not worshipped.

The nearest approach that they ever came to worshipping *any* object was that of their dead shaman. They prayed to him for long life and success in their enterprises. In the morning they would take a mouthful of water, spit it out and pray. When in danger of drowning they would pray to him for deliverance. Not only would they thus pray to him, but to things that once belonged to him. This was nothing less than fetishism, and to this extent was practised by them.

"The aborigines, where not brought into contact with government schools and missionaries, still retain their system of fetish worship, being very much under the control of their medicine men, who pretend to influence the demons of the spirit world, so feared by the average savage."

They believed firmly (and do yet) in the immortality of man. For this reason they put food in the fire, and food and clothing in the tomb of the dead; placed food and clothing on the housetop for those killed in war (whose spirits are supposed to live in the air), and canoes beside the deadhouses of their deceased shamans.

They believed firmly (and some do yet) in the transmigration of the soul, but not in the sense of the ancient Egyptian's belief. They believe that the soul transmigrates from relative to relative, but not from man to animals. For instance, if a nephew dies who has borne some peculiar mark (perhaps a birthmark) on his person and an aunt should afterwards give birth to a son who was similarly marked, it would be fully believed that the newly born was none other than the departed nephew and his name would be given to the child. It is in this sense that they believe in transmigration.

The place where the souls of the departed dwell is known as the " ghost's " or the " spirit's " home. The word for ghost is the same as for spirit. The word for soul is *kĭ-yă-hĭ'yă*, meaning, also, picture or shadow. When this *ki-ya-hi-ya* leaves the body, if the person dies a natural death and was not a slave, it goes to the happy region of spirits, which is thought of as being in some remote part of the earth; if he die in war, then it goes to dwell in the sky; if drowned, then it descends to a region below the plane of this earth, providing the body is recovered, but if not recovered it is captured by the *Goosh-tă-kă'* and taken back into the woods.

When a person is very unhappy in this world, his uncle or aunt comes to him and says, " You are unhappy where you are. Now come with me." Then the person dies and goes to the happy region where spirits are satisfied.

According to tradition, one soul came back from the spirit-land to tell the living just how they should act toward the dead, or departed spirits. Weapons must be buried with them that they may protect themselves against wild beasts and enemies; gloves and moccasins that they may protect their hands and feet against devilclubs and briars; and water to quench their thirst. When the fire crackles, spirits are hungry and calling for food. Then food must be put into the fire. Songs must be sung to lead the soul. Feasts must be given as a benefit to the spirits. Believing firmly in this, the Thlinget endeavours to carry it out. New rifles are buried with the dead as weapons of defence for the spirit. The houses in the spirit-land are named the same as the name of each one's deadhouse in this world.

Their great concern has been to propitiate the powers which they believed had power to harm them or give them success. These powers were not imaginary deities, but their totemic imaginary magnified animals to which they assigned attributes appertaining to deity. The patron bird of the Crow phratry is not the small crow or raven which we see flying about, but a mammoth imaginary creature of that species possessed with great strength and full of cunning and wisdom. Other invisible powers which they sought to appease were the spirits that they believed existed about them in almost untold numbers.

The shaman was believed not only to possess supernatural power in himself, but to be in communication with the unseen powers and have influence with them. For this reason his services were sought and he himself placated.

We have been able to find no term in their language to indicate that they had any idea of a Supreme Being such as God. The term they now use to designate the Supreme Being is *De-ke* (up) *On-Kowa* (Chief); that is, the Chief-above (God). This word was evidently coined after they had learned, through the missionaries, about God.

"The Alaskans believe in the existence of a Supreme Being. They call him Teki-Ankaose. He lives on the summit of a mountain, an arctic Olympus, where a fresh breeze is always blowing."

This fanciful writer would give the impression that this belief was original with them. His "Teki-Ankaose" is clearly the native's De-ke-Onkowa (the-up-chief). His "arctic Olympus" is a stretch of his own imagination. The Thlingets are many hundred miles from the Arctic regions, and yet he uses, as near as he knows how, their term for the Supreme Being. The unvarnished truth is that so far as we have been able to learn, through years of research, they had no idea of a deity like God until they were taught it.

A Hydah reports that his people believe in a Supreme Being. He does not say, however, that this belief was original with them. He merely affirms that they have long believed this. That may be so and the belief nevertheless be an adopted one.

Owing to their belief in the existence of a limitless number of spirits, the Thlingets have a very interesting cosmology. The sun and the moon, as well as the earth, are the abodes of numberless spirits; they are in the woods, around lakes, along

services

eir lan-
a of a
ey now
te (up)
(God).
ey had
lod.
e of a
kaose.
arctic
blow-

ession
His
De-ke-
pus ''
Thlin-
Arctic
s how,
nvar-
able
ad no
ht it.
in a
that
erely
That
e an

imit-
very
oon,
rless
long

A TROUT STREAM

trails, in the water, rocks, snow, and in every
other object. For this reason all things are conjured and nothing is contemptuously referred to.
All things have eyes and ears through the spirits
that inhabit them. Hence the caution that people
observe when speaking about them.

They are careful what they say about the moon.
Two girls were once carried off by it because they
remarked, as they were going after water, " That
moon looks just like our grandmother's labret."
Immediately they were taken up into the moon,
and the one who made the remark was broken
to pieces. The other can still be seen, in the
moon, holding her bucket.

People in earlier times grasped at shadows cast
by the sun, and would ask, after blowing on their
hands, " Let me have luck."

The sea was implored for all sorts of things,
but particularly for sea-otter, as its fur is so very
valuable. Big waves were propitiated by putting
" black raven," charcoal, on them. When this
was done, the one doing it would say, " I have
put this on you. Please stop."

The wind was talked to to induce it to moderate
or cease. Sometimes a piece of fish was thrown
to it. When it blew very hard it was said that
some one had been talking about the wolverine,
as it was believed that this animal had special
control over the north wind.

When in the neighbourhood of a glacier or big
iceberg the Thlingets always talked to it, saying,
" My son's daughter, be very careful. You might
come down on us."

As the Russians first discovered and colonized
Alaska, they were the first to introduce the Christian religion to the natives. The Græco-Russian

church was in Alaska nearly a century before any other church entered the field. Its operations were confined principally to the coast tribes. In the communities where their churches were built, the priests enrolled all the natives as members. During this long century of missionary effort, this church, if we are to believe the statements of able historians on Alaska, did little to reclaim the natives from vice, immorality and heathenism.

"It must be admitted," says Bancroft, "that the Greek [Russian] church was a failure throughout Russian America." Minor W. Bruce, an American writer whom no one can charge with being biased against the Russians, bears witness to the same truth, and Golovin, a Russian writer, bears similar testimony.

Judging from the conditions in which the natives were found when Alaska was turned over to the United States, the statements of these writers would seem to be just.

The Russian church has continued to labour with the natives, and with those of their own nationality, down to the present day. For whatever good has accrued to the natives in the last half century through the churches, it is entitled to its share of credit in the work. Whatever might have been the lives of earlier priests of that faith, those with whom we have been personally acquainted and beside whom we have laboured, have been men of good character and loyal to their work, living lives, so far as we know, beyond reproach.

The first religious work among any of the Thlingets was at Sitka in the year 1817, when the Russians built a church there.

fore any
perations
ibes. In
ere built,
members.
y effort,
atements
reclaim
heathen-

t, " that
through-
ruce, an
rge with
witness
n writer,

the na-
over to
writers

labour
own na-
or what-
the last
entitled
Vhatever
priests
een per-
have la-
ter and
r as we

of the
7, when

The first Protestant service held in Alaska by an American after the purchase by the United States was held by an army chaplain at Sitka, October 13, 1867. This was for white people and not for the natives.

No religious work was instituted among the natives by any Protestant church until ten years after the American occupation.

Missions for the natives over in British Columbia on the border line of Alaska had been established by Protestants some years previous to any work being done for the aborigines in the former country. Notable among these was the mission at Metlakhatla. That work has been so long in the public eye that no word that could be said here would in anywise raise it in the public esteem. The results of the life-long labours of Mr. William Duncan with the Metlakhatla natives are marvellous, and no tongue or pen can adequately praise such heroic self-abnegation as has been shown by this missionary to this once benighted people. It is one of the most thrilling missionary tales in the history of the world.

The first religious work instituted by any Protestant church among the Thlingets of Alaska was at Wrangell, by the Presbyterians, in 1877. The following year the same denomination opened work for the natives at Sitka. Within the first decade of missionary effort of this church several missions were established, and at the present day there are sixteen fields in southeastern Alaska alone where they are doing effective work.

Some years after the Presbyterian Church opened its work for the Thlingets, other denominations entered the field, notably the Friends, the Episcopalians, and the Salvation Army. As has

been said, the Russian Church has been in th
field since 1817.

What has been the result of this religious effor
among the natives? We will let men who cann
be charged with being biased in favour of th
church answer first.

It could never be justly said that the Hon. A
P. Swineford, once Governor of Alaska, was pai
tial to the church. In his book on Alaska, w
read, " The superstitions which formerly pre
vailed among these people have to a great exter
been eradicated through the influence and teacl
ings of the Christian missionaries."

" By the united efforts of the officials of th
civil government and the missionaries this ba
barous practice [witchcraft] has been practicall
broken up. Some of the shamans have been sul
jected to summary punishment, in cases wher
the law could not readily be invoked; others hav
been indicted and convicted, and this, togethe
with the teachings of the missionaries, has serve
to practically eradicate from among them th
chief superstition to which they were for cer
turies the abject slaves."

We were not personally acquainted with M. N
Ballou, as we were with the Hon. A. P. Swin
ford, but, judging from the tone of his book, w
would not take him as having any bias towar
the church. In "Alaska," we read: "With
the last twenty years greater intelligence has bee
shown, in part through missionaries,—self-sacr
ficing and devout men,—who have sought by the
teachings to abolish the wild superstitions of th
natives, together with their cruel rights of shama
ism."

" The self-abnegation and conscientious labor

of these people [missionaries] are truly worthy of all commendation."

" We believe the Training School at Sitka exercises a much higher civilizing influence, where the simplest Christian principles are taught, combined with common school studies, and where instruction is given in the daily industries of life."

Bancroft was an impartial historian. We read in his " History of Alaska," " For several years Protestant missionaries of several denominations, and especially the Presbyterians, have, amid great discouragements, laboured earnestly, and not in vain, to introduce their faith among the natives of Alaska. Meanwhile their efforts in the cause of education have been no less persistent."

It cannot be said that Minor W. Bruce is a partisan of the Church, yet in his " Alaska " he pays a splendid tribute to the work of the missionaries.

In the October (1906) number of the " Boston Alaskan," which is not a church periodical, we read words of commendation of the church for its part in civilizing the natives.

A few letters from natives who have been in the mission schools will testify as to the results of religious work among them: " School life is for the young. Young people have good times during their school days, but we young people go to school, not only to have a good time, but to learn what is right, and to do good, and to talk English. We are here in school so that we may have better lives when we go away from here. So we must not idle away our time, but we must work, and use our time well. We must try to learn all we can to tell our companions, who have not been to school, about this good life. I try to

keep it. I shall never forget it. This is the most
precious time of our life. So we must keep it in
our head.

"Why is it we have school life? Well, we
Thlinget people never had schools among us before, and we didn't know how to live right; now
we have teachers to teach us how. It is in school
we are getting strong. When we grow up, we will
be the leaders of our people. I don't think they
know anything about the good life. No, they
don't; only we know, so we must tell them about
it." (Mary R. Kadashan, a Chilkat.)

"My Dear Friend:—

"I will tell you what I think all time. Father
says nine years old me. I thank you for you pay
for me my teacher says. My uncle says I have to
stay here twenty years. I don't want more than
five years. My father is dead, so I have no home.
My sister says 'Don't anywhere go you, just in
mission stay you.' My sister says when five years
gone next five year's more I'll stay.

"I am trying to get to the Third reader. I
hard study me my second Reader. I am a little
boy, but I just try to know something more so
good man me.

"Good-bye,
"Johnnie Johnson."

"I am going to consider for a few minutes the
opportunities of a young native woman of Alaska.
Of course our career in life necessarily must be
different from that of a white girl, although we
may have had the same schooling. Our home life
has been different, our environments are different
and the public does not look upon us in the same
way, but I am going to prove to you that there is

a place for us, the native girls, and a great work
for us to do; and more than that, that we are able
to support ourselves. The first opportunity the
native girl has is her schooling. . . . Here we
are instructed by our teachers about housekeeping, sewing, cooking and dressmaking; all these
things help us to make our living. . . .

" A young lady may be useful in many ways.
She may be used as a school-teacher in the government schools, or as a nurse to help to stamp out
the consumption from among our own people. We
have several cases of girls who have done this and
are making a success.

" There is no nobler work for a girl than that
of improving the conditions of a home, for on
the home depends the advancement of the people.
Surely education and instruction has brought
about a marked change in our homes and mode of
living." (Fanny Phillips, a native of Chilkat.)

We have many other letters from natives which
might be submitted to show how they appreciate
the efforts of educational and religious workers
among them.

A writer in a periodical says, " The Indians
[Alaskans] are getting a better hold every year
on the principles of Christianity. They are emphatically in earnest about it, and as a consequence
there has been great improvement. Their critics
fail to appreciate that they are expected to do in
a few years what has taken the Anglo-Saxon
1,200 years to accomplish. It may be said to the
credit of the Indians that they have progressed
much more rapidly than did the Anglo-Saxon.

" We find among them even to-day men of as
high ideas of Christian life as are found among
white people in the older communities. The work

that is being done among them is bearing fruit in genuine Christian men and women.''

We could multiply such testimony as we have now submitted, but the limitations of our work will not permit it.

Only the ignorant, the thoughtless, or the vicious will be heard condemning and speaking contemptuously of the work of teachers and missionaries.

No class of men and women are more keenly aware of their limitations or more deeply deplore the fact that the natives are not as a whole on a much higher plane of life, than the missionaries. But as Rome was not built in a day, nor the English race evolved in a week, so they know that it takes time to lift a savage to a high plane of civilization. And what is more, if the vicious of their own race did not impose so many obstacles, even this could be done much quicker than it is.

XXIV

EDUCATION

TEN years rolled away after the American occupation of Alaska before anything was done by our government or by other agency for the education of the natives of the country. The initial move in this direction was made by the Presbyterian Church, the first denomination to enter Alaska after its purchase by the United States.

"Within less than a decade [from the beginning of missionary effort in Alaska] more has been done by this society [Presbyterian Board of Missions] to advance the cause of education in Alaska than was otherwise accomplished during all the years of Russian domination."

"Were it not for the efforts of the Board of Missions [Presbyterian], there would probably have been no efficient school, and perhaps no school of any kind, in the territory, apart from those maintained by the Alaska Commercial Company " (at St. Paul and St. George islands in the Bering Sea).

In a letter dated December 31, 1882, Dr. Sheldon Jackson stated that there were " seven good English schools in the Alexander Archipelago, six of which were maintained at the expense of the Board [Presbyterian], three of them having boarding and industrial departments."

The first school for the Thlingets was estab-

MICROCOPY RESOLUTION TEST CHART

(ANSI and ISO TEST CHART No. 2)

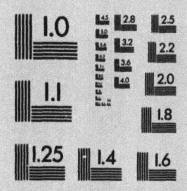

lished in the year 1877 at Wrangell under the auspices of the Presbyterian Church, and in connection with its mission at that place. Mrs. A. R. McFarland of that church, the first Protestant missionary to the natives of Alaska, was the teacher. She found the people groping after the light. A little band of aspiring natives who had come to Wrangell from Port Simpson, B. C., where they had received some education, were zealously doing what they could to impart their knowledge to their fellow-men of the former place. Thus the missionary found the soil prepared for sowing the seeds of education among the Thlingets.

By 1882 six schools had been established at different places among the Thlingets by the same agency.

As fast as new missions opened up, schools were established in connection with them. For the first decade, after the Presbyterian Church entered Alaska, it alone cared for the education of the natives.

"American governmental control left to absolute neglect for eighteen years the important question of education [of the natives of Alaska] . . . . Stimulated by appeals from officers of the army, American missionary societies were not entirely neglectful of Alaska's necessities, and in 1877 the Presbyterians, through their agent, Dr. Sheldon Jackson, established schools in southeastern Alaska, their example being soon followed by other missionary societies."

According to the same authority (Greely) the government did not assume its duties in the education of the natives until it was "finally forced by public opinion" to do so.

In 1885 the Secretary of the Interior called the attention of the Commissioner of Education to the provision made by law for the education of children in Alaska, regardless of race.

After incessant appeals Congress appropriated the niggardly sum of twenty-five thousand dollars for education in the territory. Having no school plant of its own, this appropriation was given over to the missions, and government contracted with them to look after the education of the natives in particular. The missions " generously supplemented the deficient support of the nation."

For a period of ten years after making this feeble effort, to do something for the education of the natives, nothing better was done.

Schoolhouses were finally built, practically in every village. Only the rudiments of English were taught. No industrial training whatever was given in these government schools down to the year 1908. The only training of this kind had been in connection with the mission schools. The leading industrial training school of the country is that of Sitka conducted by the Women's Board of Home Missions of the Presbyterian Church. This institution has exerted greater educational influence on the natives than all other agencies put together. It was established in 1880, and more natives have received instruction here than at any other institution. Children from all over the country enter it, and in no year in its history could it begin to receive all applicants for admission. Many natives have been doomed to a life of ignorance by our government's failure to provide education for them. For years the school could receive applicants for admission only as it

dismissed its graduates and those who had ful-
filled their period of contract, and thus made room
for new pupils.

It is a burning shame that our government did
not establish, years ago, a well-equipped training
school for the natives of Alaska. Nor does it
become any one to belittle the work the missions
have done because they do not find the natives
fully enlightened and emancipated from their old
customs. Had it not been for the missions they
would be in dense ignorance to this day for all
effort that the government has made.

" The Sitka Industrial School is the most interesting feature of the town [Sitka], because
one cannot fail to realize how much good it is
accomplishing in the way of practical civilization
and real education among the natives. At this
writing there are nearly one hundred boys, and
about sixty girls and young women, who are under
the parental care of the institution. The teaching
force consists of a dozen earnest workers, mostly
ladies from the Eastern States. Besides the
ordinary English branches taught in the school,
the girls are trained to cook, wash, iron, sew,
knit and to make their own clothes. The boys
are taught carpentry, house-building, cabinet-
making, blacksmithing, boat-building, shoemaking
and other industries. The work of the school is
so arranged that each boy and girl attends school
half a day, and works half a day. The results
thus brought about are admirable. Fifteen different tribes are represented in this Sitka Industrial School. English-speaking young natives who
have been trained here readily obtain good wages
at the mines, in the fish-canneries, and wherever
they apply for employment among the white resi-

had ful-
ade room

ment did
training
does it
missions
natives
their old
ns they
for all

nost in-
because
od it is
ilization
At this
ys, and
e under
eaching
mostly
les the
school,
n, sew,
ie boys
abinet-
making
hool is
school
results
en dif-
Indus-
es who
wages
erever
e resi-

dents of the Territory, while their influence with
their tribes is very great." *

The Hon. A. P. Swineford and other reliable
writers on Alaska bear testimony to the merits of
this institution. He who has only criticism to
offer because the missions have not already lifted
every native to an absolute state of perfection is
both unreasonable and unjust. The missions have
done their best with the means at their command.
But the very best of their schools were, for lack
of money, poorly equipped.

The government has the people's money to be
applied to such work. We pay money into its
coffers in duties, taxes, licenses, etc., and on top
of that go down into our pockets for money to
build industrial and other schools that it is the
duty of the government to provide. Thousands
of dollars are diverted every year from the spiritual interests of the church to minister to the tem-
poral welfare of men. The care of some of these
interests has been assumed by the church because
the government has not made adequate provision
for them. Schools, hospitals, orphanages, homes
for the indigent and similar institutions should be
maintained, if not conducted and controlled, by the
government.

Whose children are these that enter schools,
whose sick that enter hospitals, whose orphans
that enter orphanages, whose indigent and helpless that need homes of refuge and care? The
government's. Perhaps not five per cent of them
are within the pale of the church. And yet the
church is supposed to add to its financial burdens
the support of such institutions and in many instances is doing it without receiving contributions

* "Alaska," by Ballou, page 306.

from the non-church classes, while all are con
tributing to the government. A small part of th
public money wasted on foolish functions, nava
displays and useless court procedures would mor
than maintain all such needed institutions.

The new Presbyterian Mission plant in Sitk
is an institution in which we may take a just pride
It was built at a cost of about one hundred thou
sand dollars, is fully equipped for its work an
has a very efficient corps of instructors. It i
the only industrial training school of its kind an
of any pretensions in the country. The churc
that built it should have the everlasting gratitud
of the natives and of the white citizens of th
country who have the best interests of the lan
at heart.

The government is now trying to graft indus
trial training on to its ordinary day schools with
out supplying competent trainers. Wome
teachers who know little or nothing about indus
tries for men are expected to teach such in con
nection with all their other school work. This i
no reflection on the noble band of school teacher
in the native schools of Alaska. They are wel
fitted to teach what they should be expected t
teach, the English branches, kindergarten an
sloyd work. But for the government to suppos
for one moment that the present system is all tha
is required to train the natives in the variou
industries of life, or that it takes the place of
well-equipped industrial training school, is th
sheerest nonsense. The teachers under the pres
ent system do the best they can, but they ar
overloaded and assigned tasks beyond their abilit
to meet.

The natives show an aptitude in acquiring an

mastering trades which is little less than surprising. With little or no training in carpentry they build their own houses and many of them their boats. Some do first-class work. Many of them are skilled carvers. What trade could they not master, and that well, if they only had competent and sufficient instruction?

What they get from the mission and government schools is good so far as it goes. But it is deficient.

The trades which apply to their own country, such as carpentry, boat-building, blacksmithing, tinning, plumbing, mining and others should be taught the native youth, and dressmaking and the domestic sciences to the girls. And this should be done by the government through such an industrial system as it carries on at Carlisle, Pennsylvania, or at Chemawa, Oregon. Playing at the education of the natives of Alaska by the government should come to an end, and something real and substantial be given them.

The progress which they have made under so deficient a system shows what could be done under an efficient one. In spite of their disadvantages and the poor equipment for training, we have some who are now school-teachers, assistants to ministers, skilled miners, boat-builders, blacksmiths, silversmiths, carpenters and shoemakers among the men, and good dressmakers and housekeepers among the girls and women. But they are indebted to the church more than to any other institution for these acquirements.

Even the few who have gone to the government schools in the States were prepared by the churches to enter these schools and, in most cases, sent by them.

They should have helpful opportunities in thei
own country. They are bound to live among thei
own people and they should be prepared to d·
their best for the good of their people.

The climate of the States is not conducive t·
their health. The wide separation from thei
kindred produces pining and homesickness whic
pave the way for disease. No people on earth ar
more attached to home than these natives. Home
sickness, therefore, is a common malady wit
them. If they stay through the contract perio·
of five or ten years, as required by the school
they grow away from home-life and when the
return they are out of sympathy with it and n
longer contented. Their people notice the chang·
of feeling, and an estrangement between the
follows. If their training had been in the mids
of their people such estrangements would no
take place.

It should be borne well in mind that the native
of Alaska will stick to their own country until th
race has expired. No considerable number o
them will ever settle in the States. Alaska i
where they must fight their battles for a liveli
hood. Nothing should be done to break th
Alaskan's attachment to his country or to mak
him discontented with it and his people. H·
should be encouraged to use his education for th
enlightenment and amelioration of his people
His education and training, therefore, should b
given him in his own land.

We have known several who were educated i
the States and were wholly unhappy after returr
ing to Alaska. Had their education been cor
ducted in their own country they would not hav
been thus weaned away from it. This would b

all right if there were any hope of the white race assimilating them, and if they were not needed to help elevate their own people as a whole. But with this feeling they sometimes drift off to live an isolated life, away from all relatives, and their relatives lose entirely any elevating influence they might exert upon them were they among them.

As we write, we have in mind a graduate of one of our schools in the States. She came back to her people but was discontented. She soon returned to the States and is now employed there. This separates her entirely from her relatives, and her education has no bearing on their elevation.

Of course we are glad when they have reached that stage of life where they are dissatisfied with the way their ancestors have lived. And, furthermore, we are glad when those who have been in our schools and return home do not wish to conform to the common native life. But we would like to see more of them using their education and attainments for the uplift of their own people.

"The natives almost universally welcome and gladly improve the advantages offered them for instruction, especially as regards their children. Many individual cases with which the author became acquainted were of much more than ordinary interest; indeed, it was quite touching to observe the eagerness of young natives to gain intellectual culture. Surely this incentive is worthy of all encouragement."

Under their limited opportunities many of them now speak the English well and have a fair knowledge of reading and writing. Had they better educational facilities there is no reason why some of them, at least, could not take their places as edu-

cators by the side of white merchants, pr
sional men and educators.

Our appeal, therefore, is that our govern
give them better educational opportunities.

He who writes of the natives of Alaska a
eration hence will have a different story to
at least in part, than is told in these pages. E
year sees changes in the lives and manner
these people. It is no wild prophesying to pr
that in another generation the entire popul
will be speaking English. The leaven is worl
and in a few years, at the most, the entire l
will be leavened. This will mean a higher p
of life for the natives.

ants, profes-

government
ities.
laska a gen-
tory to tell,
ges. Every
manners of
g to predict
population
is working,
entire lump
igher plane

MAP OF
ALASKA

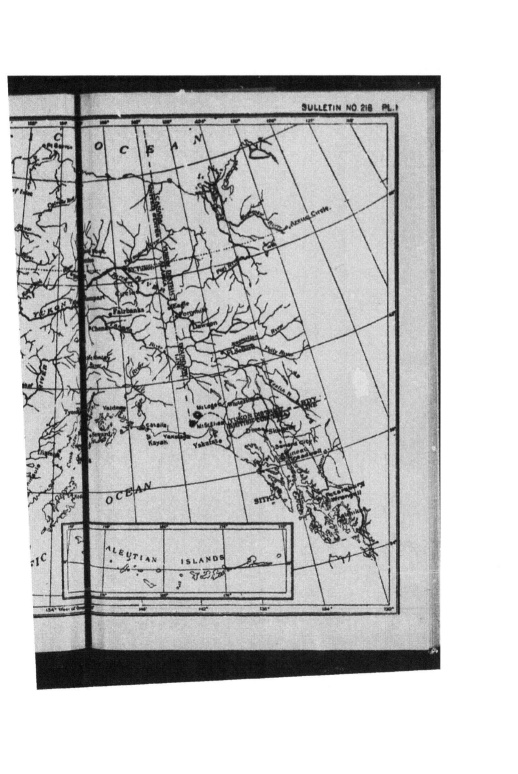

INDEX

Abalone, 70
Aborigines, 23, 31, 32
Abortion, 219
Adz, 79, 177
Affection, 99
Al-ak-shak, 17
Alaska, 17, 18, 19, 20, 21
Alaskans, 28, 30
Aleutian Islands, 20
Aleuts, 23, 24, 113
Amusements, 100, 204, 205
Ancestor Worship, 232
Ancestry, 173
Angoon, 143, 195
Animals, 107, 164, 232, 233
Appearance, 64
Archipelago, 18
Arctander, J. W., 32
Area, 18
Art, 175, 177
Article, 40
Asia, 32
Asiatics, 31
Atlas (old woman), 186
Auks, 25, 26
Aunt, 39
Aurora Borealis, 163
Authority, 44, 61

Ballou, M. M., 53, 65, 68, 216, 217, 225, 227, 232, 240, 249
Bancroft, H. H., 32, 116, 216, 217, 223, 238, 241
Banquets, 111
Basketry, 76, 85-91
Basket-weaving, 89
Bath, 227
Beaches, 53
Bead-work, 78
Bear, 74
Bear Totem, 170, 171

Beauty, 70, 131
Beaver, 185-6
Berries, 20, 108-9, 159, 172
Birds, 21
Birth, 45, 161-2
Biting, 50
Boston, 24
Boston Alaskan, 241
Blanket, 64, 76
Blarney Stone, 191
Bleeding, 226
Blindness, 230
Bluejay, 187
Bracelets, 67, 68
Brass Band, 203
Bridegroom, 209
Brother, 38
Bruce, Minor W., 19, 28, 181, 238, 241
Burial, 118, 136, 137, 147, etc.

Camps, 59
Canada, 17
Canneries, 2, 72
Canoe, 26, 79
Canoe-building 78, 79
Canoe-racing, 81
Carving, 75
Caste, 44, 56, 59, 116, 117, 118, 173, 193
Celery, 110
Changes, 62, 254
Chant, 143, 160, 204
Character, 17, 21
Charms, 163
Chastity, 214, 215
Chich'g, 173
Chief, 56, 61, 115, 139, 201, 236
Children, 44, 45, 60, 200
Chilkat River, 156, 165, 166, 191
Chilkats, 25, 26, 82, 115

255

Chinese, 28, 73
Chinook, 36, 43
Christianity, 243
Chuk-a-nady, 25
Chukchi, 31, 32
Church, 63, 238, 239, 240, 241
Citizenship, 42
Civilization, 244
Claims, 86, 149
Clans, 25, 170, 178, 179
Classes, 61
Climate, 19, 229
Clothes, 64
Coastline, 18
Community, 53
Compensation, 200
Conflicts, 115
Congress, 247
Consumption, 221-3
Contagion, 223
Contempt, 95
Cooking, 48, 111
Cordage, 73
Corruptions, 36
Cosmology, 236-7
Cottages, 57
Crabapples, 109
Crafty, 96
Creation, 184
Creator, 184
Cremation, 119, 150, 151, 153
Crests, 25, 169, 175, 179
Crime, 45, 193, 217, 218
Crow, 25, 69, 77, 165, 170, 171, 172, 182-3, 235
Cunning, 97
Customs, 33, 112

Dall, Wm. H., 28, 46, 170, 172
Dance-halls, 205
Dancing, 143-4
Damages, 173, 195
Darwinians, 172
Da-se-ton, 185
Davis, Samuel, 181
Dead-houses, 119, 137
Death, 135, 137
Debauchery, 215, 216
Deer, 40

Deformities, 230
Degeneracy, 34
Deity, 231, 233, 235
De-ke-onkowa, 236
Delicacies, 107
Delivery, 46
Demonologists, 231
Designs, 121, 175
Devilfish, 123, 188
Diseases, 154, 221, etc.
Disgrace, 126, 213
Divisions, 25, 170-1
Dogs, 49, 151, 209
Dog-salmon, 103
Domestic Life, 47
Dose, 229
Douglas, 25, 198
Dowry, 127, 129, 201
Doxology, 39
Dreams, 166
Dress, 64
Drowning, 165, 199
Drum, 142, 144, 160, 161, 20
Ducks, 108
Duk-dain-ton, 25
Duk-la-wady, 25
Duncan, Wm., 42, 172, 239
Dyes, 88, 89, 121

Eagle, 122, 165, 170, 178, 19
Earrings, 66, 67, 144
Earthquake, 186
Edgecumbe, 191
Education, 245
Embalming, 151
Emblems, 35, 169
Emmons, G. T., 86
Endurance, 99
English, 36, 37, 38, 40, 41, 24(254
Enlightenment, 22
Enterprise, 82, 83
Eskimo, 17, 23, 24
Ethics, 212, 214
Evil Spirits, 162, 232

Face-painting, 69
False Teeth, 210-11
Families, 23, 25
Family, 45, 47

Fasting, 140, 155, 228
Father, 37, 44
Feasts, 59, 60, 135, 150, 204, 235
Fetich, 158, 233
Feuds, 114, 139
Fibre, 73
Fickle, 98
Fight at Hootz-na-oo, 200
Finery, 65
Fish, 21, 103
Fisheries, 22
Fishing, 72
Fish-traps, 73
Flags, 141, 206
Flood, 188
Flour, 111
Flowers, 20
Fluency, 101
Folk-lore, 181
Fowl, 108
Freaks, 230
Frobese, J. E., 171
Frog, 170, 171, 180
Fruits, 109
Furs, 74

Gambling, 122
Gambling Sticks, 122, 123
Games, 205-6
Genealogy, 175
Gender, 40
Generic, 40
Generosity, 190
Ghost, 165, 232
Giant, 184
Giving, 199-200, 247
Glacier, 237
Golovin, 238
Goosh-ta-kah, 165, 232, 234
Gossiping, 50, 58
Government, 193, 229, 245
Grampus, 165, 179, 180
Gratitude, 102
Greek Church, 238
Greely, Major A. W., 248
Guests, 141, 174, 199
Gum, 110

Hagoo, 206
Haines, 25

Half-breeds, 45, 132
Halibut, 22, 72, 104
Hanega, 25
Harbours, 18
Hat, 180, 199
Headgear, 65
Heirlooms, 142, 144, 147
Herring, 22, 104, 105
Higginson, Ella, 24
High-caste, 56, 59, 68, 136, 178, 198
Hobgoblin, 165
Hoonahs, 74
Hootz, 173
Hootz-hit, 178
Hootz-na-oo, 200
Hootz-na-oos, 26, 145
Homesickness, 252
Hospital, 229
Hospitality, 99, 173
Hot, 173
Hounding, 95
Houses, 54, 55
House Totems, 189
Humour, 207
Humpbacks, 224
Hunting, 74
Husband, 44
Hutton, P. C., 222, 225
Hydaburg, 83
Hydahs, 24, 74, 83, 112, 180

Iceberg, 187
Idiocy, 224
Idolatry, 170
Idols, 169, 170
Ikt, 61, 154, etc., 233
Immorality, 213
Immortality, 234
Implements, 116
Independence, 92
Indians, 23, 28, 29
Indian Training, 243-4
Industries, 22, 72
Infanticide, 121
Insanity, 224
Islanders, 33
Islands, 18
Insults, 94
Italy, 17

Jackson, Sheldon, 17, 19, 23, 181, 246
Japanese, 20, 28, 29, 30, 31, 32, 34
Jealousy, 96, 115, 144
Jewellery, 67
Johnson, Johnny, 242
Juneau, 25, 26

Kaaka, 25
Kadashan, M. R., 242
Ka-gu-ne-e-thloot, 164
Kak-sucy, 25
Kamchatka, 31, 34
Kassan, 81
Katlian, 113
Keet, 69, 173, 179, 180
Keet-hit, 178
Killisnoo, 26, 185, 227
Kin-da-goosh, 165, 166
Klawock, 25
Kle-na-dy, 25
Klinquan, 177
Klondike, 75, 82
Kluckwan, 57, 83, 88, 117, 190, 191
Kluk-na-hudy, 25
Kok-won-ton, 25, 179-80
Koreans, 32
Kot, 88
Ko-te-a, 160

Labret, 68, 237
Land-otter, 165
Language, 24, 26, 35, etc.
Laws, 202
Legends, 140, 181, etc., 189
Levirate marriage, 129
Liabilities, 198
Life for life, 193
Lineage, 174
Liquor, 215, etc.
Llwyd, J. P. D., 30
Loans, 199
Love-potions, 164, 167
Low-caste, 59, 60, 173

Man's Totem, 171
Manumission, 118

Marriage, 124, 173, 209, 212, 213, 214
Masks, 137, 190
Massacre, 96, 113
McFarland, A. R., 246
Measles, 223
Measures, 108
Medicine-men (see Shaman)
Medicines, 167, 226
Metlakhatla, 239
Mexico, 17
Mines, 22
Mining, 73-4
Missionaries, 41, 148, 217, 240, 241
Missions, 239, 245
Mitkeen, 96
Moccasins, 76
Modesty, 146
Mongolian, 28, 30, 31
Morality, 212
Mortality, 222
Mortuary Poles, 152, 177
Mosquito, 184-5
Mother-of-baskets, 88, 115
Mountains, 18
Mourners, 147, 148
Mummies, 151
Murder, 193, 218
Museum, 178-180
Music, 203
Myths, 181

Nagon, 123
Names, 36, 37, 60
Nature Worship, 233
Naukth, 88
Navigation, 18
Negro, 33, 210
Nephew, 38, 45, 129
Niece, 45
Nicknames, 36
Norway, 17
Nouns, 38
Nursing, 226, 228
Nush-ke-ton, 25

Obligations, 138, 219
Observant, 100
Oils, 22, 104

3, 209, 212,

246

Shaman)
6

48, 217, 240,
;

, 31

52, 177

88, 115

8

33

29

219

Oolikan, 104, 105, 106, 107, 165
Omens, 162-3
On-kow-wa, 61
Ophthalmia, 224
Ordeals, 167
Origin, 27-34, 172, 184, 185
Original Beliefs, 232
Original Diseases, 224
Origin of Caste, 59
Origin of Totemism, 172
Ornamentation, 66
Orphan, 44

Packing, 75
Pappoose, 46
Paraphernalia, 61, 142, 155, 173
Parental Laxness, 47
Peritonitis, 227
Petersburg, 25
Phillips, Fanny, 243
Philter, 164
Phonograph, 207, 210
Phratries, 60, 141, 170, 17', 179
Politic, 97
Polyandry, 47
Polygamy, 120
Population, 23
Potlatches, 56, 62, 93, 135, 140, 141, 142, 143
Pottery, 78
Pott's Disease, 224
Preacher, 140
Presbyterian Church, 247
Presbyterian Mission, 57
Presbyterians, 230-47, 250
Prisoners of War, 113
Privacy, 58
Profanity, 220
Progress, 251
Pronouns, 40
Property, 93, 96, 132, 137-8, 199, 202
Prophet, 159
Protestant Church, 239-47
Protestants, 239
Public Utilities, 56, 57
Punishment, 47, 156, 202

Quarrels, 50, 58, 139
Quass, 216

Racing, 81
Rank, 50, 173
Raven, 165, 188, 204, 235
Relatives, 44
Religion, 231
Replogle, Chas., 29
Resources, 21
Responsibility, 196
Revenge, 96
Rings, 66
"Rubbers," 228
Rum, 217
Russians, 31, 113, 114, 216, 223, 237, 238

Sacrifice of Slaves, 117, 118
Sailors, 223
Salmon, 103, 104
Samhat (chief), 81
San Francisco, 19
Sanitation, 57, 225
Saw-mills, 22
School, 63, 245-51
Sculpin, 182
Seal, 74, 104, 107
Sea-otter, 74
Seaweed as Food, 110
Self-supporting, 72
Sensitiveness, 93
Sensuality, 215
Sentence, 41
Servants, 51
Settlements, 193-4
Seward, Wm. H., 29
Sewerage, 225
Sewing, 50, 76
Shacks, 54
Sha-he-he, 162
Shaman, 61, 155, 157, 159, 233
Shamanism, 154-161, 232, 235
Shame, 95, 96, 118, 213
Shark, 153
Shellfish, 108
Singing, 204
Sister, 38, 189
Sitka, 20, 24, 25, 29, 57, 201, 248

Sitkans, 24, 25, 74, 96
Sitka, Training School, 241, 248
Skagway, 25
Skoog-wa, 192
Slave, 61, 68, 92, 116, 117, 118
Slavery, 119
Smallpox, 223
Smoking, 220
Sociability, 99
Social Life, 57-8
Socials, 100, 205
Society, 59
Soldiers, 194, 216
Songs, 152, 180, 203, 204
Spawn, 106
Speech, 38, 100-1
Spirit, 119, 149, 154, 156, 159, 162, 232, 236
Spirit-land, 119, 149, 235
Spiritualism, 232
Sports, 203-6
Springs, 227
Standard of Morality, 132, 212
Status, 50
Steamboat, 210
Stikeens, 25, 29
Stolid, 98
Strangulation, 45
Sub-totems, 170-1
Suicide, 195, 218
Summer, 59
Superstitions, 125, 154, 162, 240
Supreme Being, 231, 236
Surveillance, 215
Suspicious, 83, 96
Swineford, A. P., 20, 29, 72, 216, 240, 249
Syphilis, 223

Taciturn, 59
Takoos, 25
Taku River, 117
Taste, 65
Tattooing, 69, 117, 121
Teachers, 41, 217
Temperature, 20
Theft, 217-18
Thlingets, 23, 25, 26, 33, 35, etc., 58, 59, 72

Thunder Bird, 186
Tinneh, 23, 24
Tobacco, 220
Tolth, 87
Tongass, 25
Too-da-hook, 87
Tools, 55
Toothache, 221
Torture, 156
Totem, 56, 75, 141, 233
Totemism, 168-180
Totem Poles, 133, 138, 16
    175-7
Toughening Process, 120
Tourist, 24, 28, 86, 176
Town-sites, 18, 53
Tradition, 60, 235
Traffic, 82
Traits, 33, 92
Transmigration of Soul, 234
Trapping, 74
Travel, 23, 28
Treachery, 101, 113
Treadwell, 74
Tribes, 23, 24, 25, 26, 37, 56, 1
Truth, 219
Tschak, 25, 77
Tsimpshean, 24, 32, 42
Tuberculosis, 222
Twins, 121, 162-3
Tzow (het), 180

Ulcers, 227
Uncles, 45

Vanity, 93, 120
Vegetables, 109-10
Vegetation, 20
Venereal Diseases, 223
Venison, 22
Verbs, 40
Vices, 220
Villages, 18, 53, 55
Virtue, 219
Vocabulary, 39
Volcanoes, 19

War, 112
War-canoes, 81
Washing, 49-50

86

1, 233

, 138, 168,

s, 120
176

Soul, 234

, 37, 56, 170

42

23

Washington, D. C., 20
Water System, 57
Wealth, 61
Weights, 87, 108
Whale-killer, 69
Whales, 188, 189, 190
Whale Tribe, 185
Whooping-cough, 223
Widows, 147, 152, 163, 199
Wife, 44, 50-1
Wig, 210
Willard, E. S., Mrs., 160
Winter, 59
Witch, 96, 155, 156, 157, 158

Witchcraft, 125, 154, 158, 162
Witch-medicine, 157, 158
Wolf, 170, 171, 186
Woman's Totem, 171
Word-building, 35
Worm, 190
Worm-dish, 115
Wrangell, 114

Yak, 26, 78
Yakutat, 24, 25, 113
Yalkth, 25, 69
Yalkth-hit, 178
Yana-ate, 110

PRINTED IN THE UNITED STATES OF AMERICA

JOHN T. FARIS *Author of "Men Who Made Good"*

The Alaskan Pathfinder

The Story of Sheldon Jackson for Boys. Illustrated, 12mo, cloth, net $1.00.

The story of Sheldon Jackson will appeal irresistibly to every boy. Action from the time he was, as an infant, rescued from a fire to his years' of strenuous rides through the Rockies and his long years' of service in Alaska, permeate every page of the book. Mr. Faris, with a sure hand, tells the story of this apostle of the Western Indians in clear-cut, incisive chapters which will hold the boy's attention from first to last.

G. L. WHARTON

Life of G. L. Wharton

By Mrs. Emma Richardson Wharton. Illustrated, 12mo, gilt top, cloth, net $1.25.

A biography of a pioneer missionary of the F. C. M. S., written by a devoted wife who shared the experiences of her husband in a long service in India and Australia. It is a life of unusual interest and an important addition to the annals of modern missionary effort.

MRS. LAURA DELANY GARST

A West Pointer in the Land of the Mikado

Illustrated, 12mo, cloth, net $1.25.

The story of a great life given unreservedly to the service of God in Japan—a life story representative of the best the West sends the East and typical of that missionary spirit in America which is one of the marvelous things in the growth of the Christ life in man. The Christian world will be proud of and wish to study such a record—coming generations will find here inspiration and incentive for yet greater effort and larger sacrifice.

HENRY OTIS DWIGHT

A Muslim Sir Galahad

A Present Day Story of Islam In Turkey. Net $1.00.

"The author of 'Constantinople and Its Problems,' has written an intensely interesting story of present-day Turkish life. A fascinating picture of the Mohammedan world. Recent events in the Near East make this book of unusual interest, and a better book, throwing sidelights on the Mohammedan question, could not be found."—*Pacific Presbyterian.*

ROLAND ALLEN, M.A.

Essential Missionary Principles

12mo, cloth, net $1.00.

An author new to American readers has claimed attention of students of missions through his recent thought-compelling book, *Missionary Methods—St. Paul's or Ours?* This latter volume dealing with the *principles* of missions well supplementing the volume on *methods*.

ROLAND ALLEN, M.A.   *Library of Historic Theology*

Missionary Methods : St. Paul's or Ours ?

With Introduction by Rt. Rev. Henry Whitehead, D.D., Lord Bishop of Madras. 8vo, cloth, net $1.50.

Is this book the true answer to the question as to why Christian Missions do not progress to-day as rapidly as we should like to see them doing? Dr. Allen was formerly a missionary in North China and author of "The Siege of Peking Legations" and writes from large experience. His arguments for the application of truly Pauline methods of envangelization in foreign mission fields are startling. The reader may not agree with all of his criticisms and suggestions but the discussion which will be aroused cannot fail to be helpful. It is a vigorous presentation of a profoundly important subject.

MISS MINNA G. COWAN

The Education of the Women of India

Illustrated, 12mo, cloth, net $1.25.

The subject is treated historically, philosophically and suggestively. The contributions made by the government, the East Indians themselves and the missionaries, to solving the educational problems of the country are clearly shown. The book is an important and suggestive addition to the literature of education in foreign lands, being a worthy companion volume to Miss Burton's "The Education of Women in China."

LIVINGSTON F. JONES

A Study of the Thlingets of Alaska

12mo, cloth, illustrated, net $1.50.

For twenty-one years the author has labored as a missionary representing the Presbyterian Board of Home Missions among the people about which he writes. Probably no living man is better qualified to tell about this interesting race. Hon. James Wickersham says: "Contains much that is new and valuable in respect to the social life and ancient customs of the Thlinget Indians. An interesting and valuable contribution to the ethnology of the Pacific Coast."

I. N. McCASH

The Horizon of American Missions

12mo, cloth, net $1.00.

Lectures delivered before the College of Missions. Dr. McCash has treated the subject in a broad and masterful way. The book is a distinct and timely contribution to the subject. Some of the topics treated are:—"A Historic Survey of American Missions," "A Regional Survey of L met Religious Needs," "Foreign Elements in the Equitation of American Missions," "Cities Related to the Kingdom of God," "Loyal Church Efficiency," "America Democratising the World."

MARY CLARK BARNES and DR. LEMUEL C. BARNES

The New America

Home Mission Study Course. Illustrated, 12mo, cloth, net 50c. (post. 7c.) ; paper 30c. (post. 5c.).

This, the regular text-book for the coming year is on the subject of immigration. The eminent authors are fitted for writing on this theme having given much time to studying the problem.

LAURA GEROULD CRAIG

America, God's Melting Pot

Home Mission Study Course. Illustrated, 12mo, paper, net 25c. (postage 4c.).

The subject chosen for study this year, Immigration, covers so wide a field that it was thought best to prepare a supplemental text book from an entirely different standpoint. The author has written a "parable study" which deals more with lessons and agencies than with issues and processes.

LEILA ALLEN DIMOCK

Comrades from Other Lands

Home Mission Junior Text Book. Illustrated, 12mo, paper, net 25c. (postage 4c.).

This book is complementary to the last volume in this course of study, Dr. Henry's SOME IMMIGRANT NEIGHBORS which treated of the lives and occupations of foreigners in our cities. This latter tells what the immigrants are doing in country industries. Teachers of children of from twelve to sixteen will find here material to enlist the sympathies and hold the interest of their scholars.

S. D. GORDON

Quiet Talks on Following the Christ

12mo, cloth, net 75c.

The latest volume of "Quiet Talks" radiates strength and courage for the Christian life. Of all Mr. Gordon's books there is none that grips the heart with more impelling force, bringing the reader and the truth face to face. Contents: The Lone Man Who Went Before, The Rough Road He Trod, The Pleading Call to Follow, What Following Means, Shall We Go? Finger Posts, Fellow-Followers, The Glory of the Goal.

W. L. WATKINSON, D.D.

The Gates of Dawn

Devotional Readings for a Year. With a Short Series of Prayers by Lauchlan Maclean Watt, M.A., B.D. 8vo, cloth, net $1.25.

These delightful devotional suggestions show Dr. Watkinson at his best. The meditations are rich with the illustrative and allusive qualities for which the great preacher is famous.

CLELAND BOYD McAFEE, D.D.

○ "His Peace" A Message for an Age of Doubt and Faith

16mo, boards, net 25c.

An irresistible plea for a clearer recognition of the present power of Christ in daily life.

The *Christian Advocate* says: "Dr. McAfee writes from the view of to-day's man. He sees clearly and thinks keenly, and his straightforward, manly words tend to edification."

ANNA AUSTEN McCULLOH

Sunday Reflections for the Church Year

Cloth, net $1.00; limp leather, gilt top, net $1.75.

A book of brief reflections on the collect and Scriptures for each Sunday of the church year. It is intended to help the reader to "that best of all habits of the soul, the finding each day new, in the fresh discovery of the worth and beauty of life."

J. D. JONES, M.A., B.D.

A Devotional Commentary on St. Mark I-VI. 8vo, cloth, net $1.00.

Draws out with characteristic skill the personal lessons to be derived from the Gospel. Alike on its expository and on its devotional side the work should be helpful to all who seek guidance and stimulus for a life of faith and service. It is hoped to complete the treatment of this Gospel in two volumes.

NEWELL DWIGHT HILLIS, D.D.

Lectures and Orations by Henry Ward Beecher

Collected and with Introduction by Newell Dwight Hillis. 12mo, cloth, net $1.20.

It is fitting that one who is noted for the grace, finish and eloquence of his own addresses should choose those of his predecessor which he deems worthy to be preserved, the most characteristic and the most dynamic utterances of America's greatest pulpit orator.

DAVID SWING

The Message of David Swing to His Generation Addresses and Papers, together with a Study of David Swing and His Message by Newell D. Hillis

12mo, cloth, net $1.20.

A collection of some of David Swing's greatest orations and addresses, mostly patriotic, none of which have before been published in book form. Dr. Hillis, who has gathered them together, contributes an eloquent tribute to his distinguished confrere in an Introductory "Memorial Address."

WAYNE WHIPPLE

The Story-Life of the Son of Man

8vo, illustrated, net $2.50.

Nearly a thousand stories from sacred and secular sources woven into a continuous and complete chronicle of the life of the Saviour. Story by story, the author has built up from the best that has been written, mosaic like, a vivid and attractive narrative of the life of lives. Mr. Whipple's life stories of Washington and Lincoln in the same unique form, have both been conspicuously successful books.

GAIUS GLENN ATKINS, D.D.

Pilgrims of the Lonely Road

12mo, cloth, net $1.50.

In nine chapters the author presents what he calls the "Great Books of the Spirit". Beginning with the Meditations of Marcus Aurelius, he interprets with spiritual insight and clarity of expression the Confessions of St. Augustine, Thomas à Kempis' Imitation of Christ, the Theologia Germanica, Bunyan's Pilgrim's Progress, etc.

ROSE PORTER

A Gift of Love and Loving Greetings for 365 Days

New Popular Edition. Long 16mo, net 50c.

"All the texts chosen present some expressions of God's love to man, and this indicates the significance of the title."
—*The Lutheran Observer.*

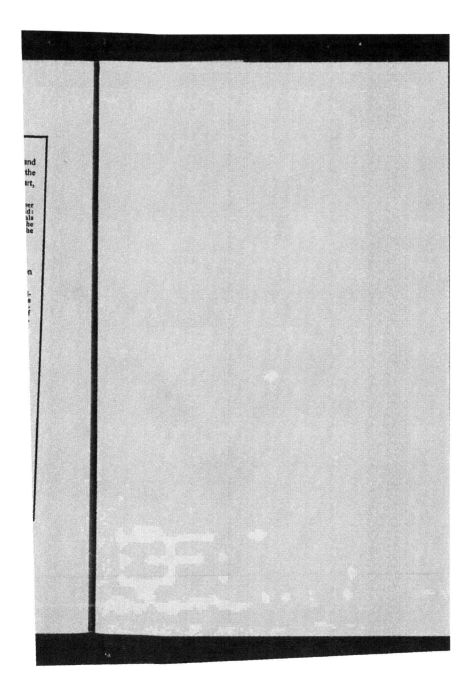